AN ARTIST'S IMPRESSIONS OF ITS ARCHITECTURE AND HISTORY

written and illustrated by Richard Grosvenor

Newport Waterfront   Richard Grosvenor
                                                                                                                    1974

Library of Congress Cataloging-in-Publication Data

Grosvenor, Richard, 1928–
    Newport : an artist's impressions of its architecture and history / written and illustrated by Richard Grosvenor.
        p. cm.
        ISBN 1-889833-34-7
        1. Architecture--Rhode Island--Newport. 2. Newport (R.I.)--History.
I. Title.
        NA735.N54 G76 2002
        720'.9745'7--dc21

                                                                        2002025611

Designers: Alyssia Newton, Laura McFadden
Printed in Singapore
Commonwealth Editions is an imprint of Memoirs Unlimited, Inc.
21 Lothrop Street, Beverly, Massachusetts 01915.
Visit our Web site at www.commonwealtheditions.com.

10 9 8 7 6 5 4 3 2 1

FOR MARGOT

Each civilized race, ancient or modern, has incarnated

its own aesthetic life and character in definite forms

of architecture. At the prevailing life motive of any epoch,

we must read its architecture as well as its literature.

—James Jackson Jarves

Vernon Court, 1898–1901, Thomas Hastings

contents

6   Foreword by Paul F. Miller
    Curator, The Preservation Society of Newport County

8   Introduction

10 Chapter 1: The Early Colonial Period

26 Chapter 2: Newport in the
    Eighteenth Century

40 Chapter 3: The New Republic Takes Root

50 Chapter 4: Newport in Transition:
    At Work and Play

66 Chapter 5: Newport in Transition:
    At Home

82 Chapter 6: Mason and Newton, Architects

96 Chapter 7: Newport and the Search for an
    American Architecture

114 Chapter 8: The Mansions of Newport's
    Gilded Age

134 Chapter 9: The Twilight of Newport's
    Golden Age

144 Appendix: Selected Architects of Newport

154 Architectural Styles

156 Maps and Illustrations

158 Acknowledgments

foreword

Revisiting the Newport of his youth, Henry James writes in *The American Scene*: "One views it as placed there, by some refinement in the scheme of nature, just as a touchstone of taste—with a beautiful little sense to read into it by a few persons, and nothing at all to be made of it, as to its essence, by most others." The visitor of today's sense of Newport's essence, so clear to James, remains generally overwhelmed by the city's dizzying concentration, spanning three hundred years, of significant domestic architecture. Nowhere else in the nation does such a comprehensive and definitive range of architectural styles exist in such a compact cluster. To the unguided eye, a passing glimpse at Newport divulges a muddled impression of seemingly disparate, but always expensive, residential structures. With *Newport: An Artist's Impressions of Its Architecture and History*, Richard Grosvenor invites the reader to uncover

Newport's timeless mood, to go out and look about town, to investigate the connected and progressive chapters of Newport's architectural evolution, much of which has been neglected all too long. His is an appeal to stroll through the "Old Town" and be charmed by the indefinable elegance of its eighteenth-century structures. The beauty of the walk will, in turn, inspire the visiting reader to continue on to the "Social Town" of the early mid-nineteenth-century, across shady lawns and timber-framed verandas. As the houses grow bigger and the gardens seem to grow smaller, we arrive at the "Town of the White Elephants," representative of America's international coming of age with the concomitant loss of a certain quaint stylistic innocence and innovation.

With the brush of an artist and the succinct narrative of a teacher, Richard Grosvenor devotes himself to the mission of illustrating and outlining the logical course of Newport's search for the proper architectural models. A lifelong resident of the city, Mr. Grosvenor takes us on a peripatetic tour of both Newport's well-known primary monuments and its lesser known, but highly influential, early villas. Richly illustrated with Mr. Grosvenor's highly evocative and original drawings, the reader will herein embark on a voyage and sketching tour revealing, in a more keenly sensed light, a sense of Newport's true essence.

Paul F. Miller

Curator

The Preservation Society of Newport County

Newport Harbor and Trinity Church

introduction

Perched on the southern end of Aquidneck Island between Narragansett Bay and the Sakonnet River, Newport occupies a unique place in American history. Founded as a haven of religious tolerance during a time of general intolerance, it was home to churchmen, but also pirates. And patriots. Citizens of Newport helped launch the American Revolution.

Perhaps Newport's most important quality is its historic focus on the arts and intellect. Artists, architects, and cultural leaders have found their way here since 1639, arriving from England, and eastern cities from New York to Baltimore,

Boston to Philadelphia. Authors Edith Wharton and Henry James both lived in Newport, though James spent only part of his childhood here. Maude Howe Elliot, Ezra Stiles, Oliver Hazard Perry, and his brother Matthew all made Newport their home. Winslow Homer lived here while he was an illustrator for *Harper's* magazine; Gilbert Stuart, famous for his portraits of George Washington, lived close by in Saunderstown. Painters of the Hudson River school, such as Albert Bierstadt, John La Farge, and John F. Kensett, recorded their impressions of the town.

Gilbert Stuart, self-portrait, courtesy of the Redwood Library

The architectural styles of Newport's buildings, their locations, and their many functions form a compelling history. The trail begins at the Old Stone Mill in Touro Park and winds through a Colonial heritage of small wooden houses, graceful Trinity Church, and contributions of one of the New World's first architects, Peter Harrison. It leads through the monumental, though short-lived, Greek Revival period. A reaction to more than a century of classicism may be seen in the towered and crenellated eccentricities of the Victorian era. These organic houses were populated by some of America's most intellectual families.

Famed on Newport's architectural trail, of course, stand the wild, ostentatious palaces built during the height of the Gilded Age. Nor are they the end of architectural activity in Newport: the twentieth century brought the city much talent, from Bruce Price, William Allen Delano, Irving Gill, all the way to modern-day architect Robert Stern. Many architects at work today are emerging to make their mark in architectural annals; The Newport Collaborative, William L. Burgin, Richard Long, and Estes Twombly Architects, just to name a few. Many are forward-looking in devoting a lot of energy to adaptive reuse of architectural treasures instead of replacing them.

—Richard Grosvenor

the early colonial period

Newport seems to exist in a world apart. It takes only a little while for the visitor to realize

that the city's unique qualities were built into it by time and space. So much history still lives

within the narrow girdle of Aquidneck Island—a finite, exquisitely beautiful place. And that

history is plainly legible on the varied surfaces of Newport's homes and public buildings, dating

back to the seventeenth century—perhaps even further back.

THE OLD STONE MILL

This tower of rough stonework (in Touro Park, just off Bellevue Avenue and north of Memorial Boulevard) has remained a mystery for generations of Newporters. Little is known about the origin of this ruin, except that it is located on land that belonged to Governor Benedict Arnold (grandfather of the Revolutionary War traitor) in the 1650s, and that he mentions it in a letter as his "stone-built wind mill." Later, it served as the base for a windmill that ground corn during the days just before and during the Revolution. The Old Stone Mill bears the marks of a sophistication uncommon to its time and place in the New World. The eight columns are aligned to the cardinal points of the compass, and the distance between columns is an even number of Scandinavian feet. A romantic theory, perhaps initiated by Henry Wadsworth Longfellow, has it that Vikings built the mill. Another theory proposes the builders were very accomplished (and perhaps members of the Knights Templar), owing to the resemblance between the mill's structure (a round tower and eight columns oriented to points on the compass) and the sepulcher built in Jerusalem. Many more theories about its origin have been spelled out in books now on the shelves of Newport's Redwood Library. All we know for certain is that the tower is one of Newport's oldest structures—if not *the* oldest.

the growth of the early city

In the seventeenth century, a small river flowed down Tanner Street, now Dr. Marcus Wheatland Boulevard. The stream's source was a small pond at the site of the current Pond Avenue. This river powered several mills; as the street's name implies, they were *tanning* mills. At the end of Tanner Street, the river bent to the right at what is now River Lane, flowed by the prison, crossed Thames Street, and emptied into the cove.

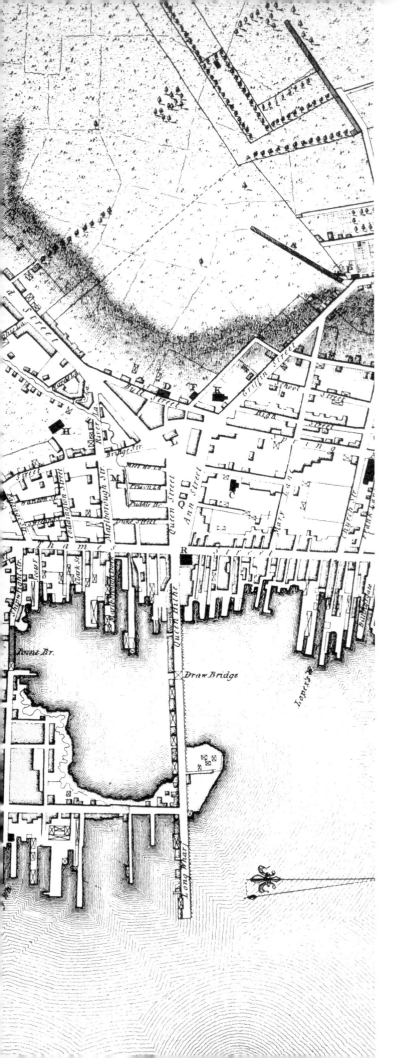

The shapes of Newport's buildings and streets are signs of practical decisions made by many individuals over centuries. For example, some of the straight streets in Kay and Catherine Streets are the sites of old ropewalks—long buildings in which ropes and cordage for ships were fashioned.

Wheels at each end of a ropewalk twisted long fibers stretched between them. The longer the distance between the wheels, the longer the piece of line manufactured. In Newport, one ropewalk was $1/4$ mile long. Communication from one end to the other usually involved shouting to other workers down the line. The ropewalks were noted for their noise, their smell (tar was used in abundance), and their tendency to burn. Because they were fire hazards, walks were usually relegated to the outskirts. Not everyone found them unattractive, however. Newport deacon Samuel Williams wrote in 1830:

> *Do not let me forget . . . the long rambling rope walks with their magical perspective, delicious scent of hempen cordage, and the drowsy drone of the turning wheel hundreds of feet off, and the sweet sunlight streaming in through the olden shutters.*

Richard Champlin tells us:

> *Deacon Williams lived on Elizabeth Street and owned all the land between Touro Synagogue and the Jewish*

cemetery. He constructed two ropewalks, one roughly where Whitfield Place is. The other formed the roadbed of Kay Street. Other ropewalks occupied Callender Avenue in the area behind Dr. Marcus Wheatland Boulevard; Tew's Court, off Old Beach Road; and a walk called Brinley's at the west end of Catherine Street.

Spring Street

Winding north, roughly parallel to Thames Street, Spring Street's course is not as straight as others that once housed ropewalks. It probably owes its direction to the wandering animals that created this path on their way to and from the town spring. A bronze plaque at a Texaco station near the Colony House marks the site of the now-vanished spring.

The Wanton-Lyman-Hazard House, circa 1700, 17 Broadway

architectural traditions

Newport's rich architectural history can be traced from late Medieval styles, through the classicism of Federal, Colonial, and Greek Revival periods, to the organic styles of the Victorian era. One of the city's oldest buildings is the Wanton-Lyman-Hazard House (circa 1700), at 17 Broadway. The house is important because it shows transition (away from the Gothic) to a more baroque ideal. What began as a simple structure, with a room on either side of a central chimney, was later enlarged and an elegant staircase was added.

Former owners who lent their names to the house include John G. Wanton, who purchased it at auction in 1765; then Daniel Lyman, who married Wanton's beautiful daughter Polly in 1782. Another marriage, this one between Polly and Daniel Lyman's daughter and Benjamin Hazard, sealed the triple moniker for the building.

Names aside, an early (1757) owner of the house, Tory tax collector Martin Howard, is perhaps its most celebrated. Tradition has it that a mob attacked the house during the Stamp

Act Riot of 1765, and tried to pull down the chimney. Howard fled, never to return, but the chimney remains—along with a huge kitchen fireplace and bake oven. The house is one of two seventeenth-century houses left in Newport (the other is the Bliss House.)

Colonial houses have a timbered aesthetic: Instead of the light frame construction made possible by machined wood and two-by-fours, colonial framing was often done without studs and, just as often, included roof supports of timber from felled trees. In the seventeenth century, tree-cutting equipment was adequate, but rudimentary. Both wood and nails were at a premium. Nails had to be produced laboriously and expensively by blacksmiths. The houses built were small structures, by necessity as well as tradition. Framing was basic and solid. Each piece of wood was a necessary element, joined to others with minimal use of nails. All heavy pieces were joined by mortise and tenon. When two of these pieces were fitted together, the final fastening was a wooden peg, or *trunnel*—literally a *tree nail*.

Timbers were sometimes chosen for shape, perhaps as a reflection of shipbuilding practices in the community (a timber that grew to the shape needed is stronger than a timber that is cut to fit.) Thus, it is possible to find houses whose rafters were branches angled naturally in a tree before becoming part of the roof. In colonial terms, the strength this "bent tree construction" offered was worth a little asymmetry (a jog

is plainly visible in the Wanton-Lyman-Hazard House roof, for example, owing to its underlying timber.)

The Wanton-Lyman-Hazard House shows another interesting artifact: its ungainly, plaster coved cornice, is unusually wide—perhaps in a Colonial attempt to emulate a classical design just becoming popular in England, but only seen by the colonists as illustrations.

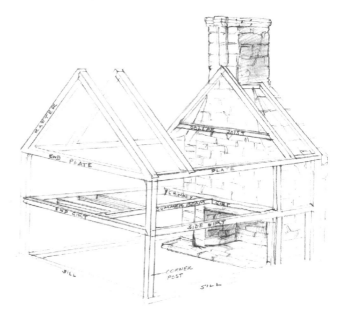

Above: Colonial framing

Left: Mortise and tenon joint

Lucina Langley House, 43 Pelham Street

Colonial buildings are easy to recognize among their nineteenth-century neighbors. The scale of the house is perhaps its most outstanding feature; it is much smaller than the styles that follow. The timber frame Lucina Langley House (43 Pelham Street) is tiny, though it served as quarters for Hessian soldiers assigned to protect British General Richard Prescott during the Revolutionary War. The general's headquarters were 50 yards away in the Bannister House, across Spring Street.

"Stone Enders," houses with stone forming the end facades, are great examples of the power that tradition exerted on design. The John Bliss House, which stands near the corner of

Bliss Road and Eustis Avenue, is reminiscent of its British antecedents, yet it is adapted to the New World's climate: The house is oriented to the north, so that its chimney forms a massive buttress to the prevailing northwest winds.

As in other late-seventeenth-century Colonial buildings, the interior spaces are compact, just adequate for a small family. The main focus of life in such a house is the hearth, which, in the case of the Bliss House, is immense. All the cooking took place here. The size speaks of the plentiful wood available on the island in the early years; in the eighteenth century, as more land was cleared, wood grew scarcer and houses were built with smaller fireplaces.

In the Bliss House, a beehive oven in the rear was used for baking bread and other foods. You can see its shape sticking out like a blister on the stone end facing Bliss Road. Inside the house, flat stones in the floor of the fire opening of the main hearth are set vertically. The spaces between the narrow faces of the stones provided a natural draft to feed the flames.

Other features of the Bliss House include the heavy framing typical of a Colonial house and a well-designed, steep stairway.

While the Bliss House is a link to the housebuilding of Europe, it also is connected with an early Newport mystery.

John Bliss House

The John Bliss House, Bliss Road

Farmer John Bliss owned a strip of land adjacent to Easton's Pond, which in the seventeenth century opened to the sea. An excavation known as the Bliss Mine ran parallel to the pond. A newspaper article of 1851 provides tantalizing speculation about the mine:

AN EXCERPT FROM THE *NEWPORT MERCURY*, SEPTEMBER 6, 1851

"The reason for calling it Bliss Mine, as far as we have been able to learn, is this: Old Mr. Bliss, who owned the tract of land where the cavern is situated, in sixteen hundred and eighty, or thereabouts, commenced digging in the cave, and employed himself in mining for years; giving out that there was gold in the quartz rock, and that he believed he would eventually strike a vein of that ore. He is said to have been a man of sound mind on every other subject, and would listen to no one who questioned the probability of his success. This is all that we actually know respecting the cavern, except that it was a haunt, about sixty years ago, of a band of thieves who infested the Island, carrying off sheep and calves. They were traced to the cave, where a number of slaughtered animals were found. Since then, the cavern has been allowed to fill up, until now it requires some bodily effort to pass from one division to the other; and, but for the late exploration [just undertaken], would have probably in a few years been completely choked up. . . .

Our own opinion is, that the cavern (probably at first a small natural one) was enlarged and the gallery built by the pirates, who in the early settlement of the country, made this Island their headquarters. . . .

But, it will be asked, how do we make this harmonize with the known facts that Mr. Bliss mined there for years? Simply thus: He is said to have been a man of strong mind on every other subject; may he not have accidently discovered the covered way leading to or from the pond; and knowing that the Island had been infested with pirates, at once conjectured that it must have been their work and that the cavern was their store house? If such a question once arose in his mind, would he not keep the secret to himself and dig quietly for supposed treasure? To mislead the inquisitive, he could not invent a better tale and at the same time confine himself to the truth, than by stating that he was mining for gold. . . ."

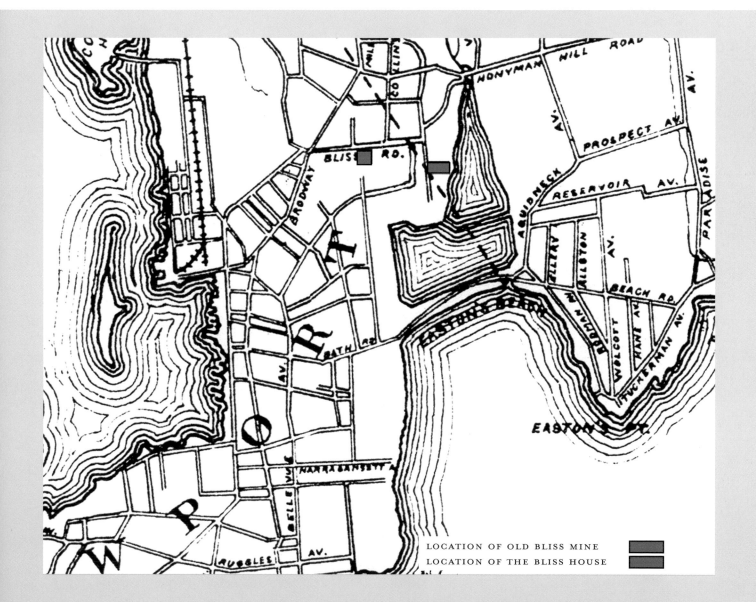

LOCATION OF OLD BLISS MINE
LOCATION OF THE BLISS HOUSE

To look at the Bliss House in today's suburban setting, it's hard to imagine the fields that once surrounded it. John Bliss trudged the road that still runs by to the north of the dwelling, and we know he took the old route to his "mine" that now ends at the Newport Water Department buildings. He would never recognize the world as it appears today, though he would still recognize his house, as it has been well cared for and preserved for close to three hundred years.

Easton's Beach, courtesy of the Newport Historical Society

Framed overhang on the Sueton Grant House,
originally called the Jeremy Clarke House

COLONIAL ROOF TYPES

The rooflines of the Colonial era are quite straightforward
and unassuming. Other features of Colonial domestic
architecture are windows sited just under the cornice and
clapboards that grow noticeably narrow as they approach
the bottom sill.

Gable Roof

Gambrel Roof

colonial domestic architecture

The framed overhang house, common in the early Colonial period, was based on similar houses in France and England as settlers in the New World remembered them. Why the overhang? Some believe its primary purpose was simply to add floor space to the second floor, especially in crowded cities. It is also possible that this design served a structural purpose: with second-story walls set beyond the perimeter of the first floor, the floor joists of the second floor were flexed, giving the whole structure a greater rigidity. The Governor Coddington House (whose lot formerly extended from the northern part of Thames Street to Farewell Street, the location of Coddington's burial ground) and the Sueton Grant House were constructed in this manner; unfortunately, both were destroyed in the nineteenth century.

The White Horse Tavern, the small clapboard building on the corner of Fairwell and Marlborough streets, now serves as

The White Horse Tavern

an elegant restaurant. It was first owned by William Mayes, a pirate who sailed as far as Madagascar in search of ships laden with riches. He established it as a tavern, and it served as a general town hall and criminal court before the Colony House was built in 1739–44. It's possible that the twenty-six pirates hanged on Gravelly Point in 1726 were tried here.

Gable-on-Hip Roof

Dutch Gambrel Roof

The gable-on-hip roof is an innovation that takes place around 1725. The Dutch gambrel on this 1771 building, the Erastus Pease House at 36 Church Street, is merely a regular gambrel with a flair.

newport in the eighteenth century

From its founding in 1639 to the beginning of the American Revolution, Newport grew from hamlet to thriving port city. Its early Colonial development was haphazard. Houses were bunched and streets planned casually, as in other early settlements in the New World. This randomness reflected the Gothic inheritance the first settlers brought with them to the New World.

In the 1700s, however, under the orderly influence of Quakers and the Enlightenment, wealthy sea captains laid out a regular grid for their streets, particularly in the Point section. (Settled later than Newport proper, the Point offered sea captains a convenient waterside location for launching and boarding their ships.) The eighteenth century also witnessed the dawn of architectural sophistication in Newport.

Trinity Church and Church Street

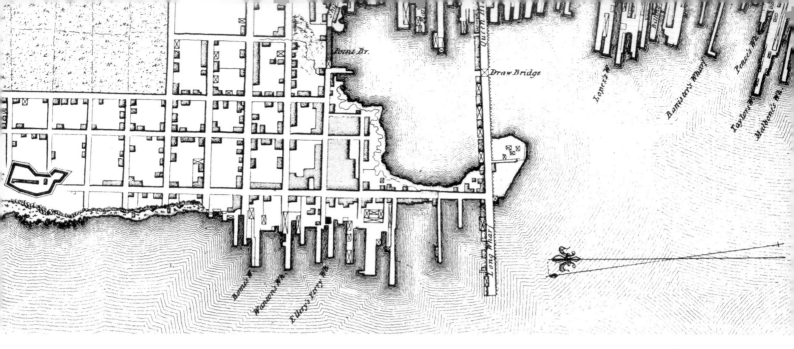

The Point Section

the point

Long Wharf, built around 1740, linked the original commercial center of the town with the Point, where eighteenth-century sea captains built their larger residences. A drawbridge spanned a small gap in the wharf, through which oceangoing traffic passed into the backwaters of the cove.

The wharf focused waterfront commerce in one location. This became the marketplace for cordwood from Maine, grain from Newport, and other cargoes. Pens on the wharves held slaves newly received from Africa. Newport was one of the largest slaving ports of that time; many of the sea captains living on the Point made their fortunes from the "triangle trade." This trading practice consisted of shipping rum to the African coast, trading it for Negro slaves, carrying the slaves to the West Indies, trading them for molasses, and, finally, carrying molasses to Rhode Island, where it was distilled into rum.

design refinements

With the increase in sea trade and of the status of sea captains, differences between the artisan's home and the captain's home became more pronounced. The Hunter House (54 Washington Street) is a good example of a wealthy captain's dwelling. It is unique in that the walls are fabricated with masonry on the inside (as opposed to simply timber)—at least, in the original half of the house. Originally, the dwelling was about half its current size. It was enlarged as the wealth of the owners increased.

Inside, the full-depth hall is divided by a monumental arch that separates the front entrance hall from the rear stair hall. Fine craftsmanship and detail abound, ranging from the carved balustrades on the staircase to the wooden columns in the drawing room, carefully painted to resemble marble. Throughout the house, simple pine boards are painted to look like more exotic varieties of wood. One room is paneled in painted rosewood, finely grained in convincing imitation of the expensive import. Such adornment was considered a great mark of taste and wealth, as was locally crafted Townsend and Goddard furniture.

The Hunter House is one of Newport's treasures. While more splendid than many, it is typical of homes of its period: It has two classical enfaced columns at the front door and its chimneys are less massive than those of earlier homes. While treasures might abound inside, eighteenth-century domestic architecture of the Colonial period remained relatively simple outside.

The Hunter House, circa 1740
(enlarged, 1758), Washington Street

richard munday, joiner

Some public buildings dating from the early 1700s are remarkable for their sophistication. This was the baroque period in England, which dates to the rebuilding of London after the disastrous fire of 1666, largely by famed architects Christopher Wren and Inigo Jones. Their designs were well-known in the colonies, where prints of many were available.

Wren's influence can be seen in Richard Munday's Trinity Church (entrances from Church Street and Mill Street), which was completed in 1726. Munday considered himself a carpenter (or joiner), not an architect, yet Trinity is perhaps Newport's most brilliant jewel. The shipbuilding trade that permeated the community was not lost on Munday, and he translated Wren's sometimes ponderous stone-building design into the grace of wooden construction. The delicate shape of the spire, perfectly formed to its function, contrasts dramatically with the earthen hues and more earth-bound shape of much of the rest of the city. Ironically, Trinity's original color may not have been white. Many of Newport's buildings were painted white only during the Greek Revival period, one hundred years after the church was completed.

Trinity Church, 1725–26, Richard Munday,
Spring Street and Church Street

The Pulpit, Trinity Church, 1726, Richard Munday

Trinity Church was built with the same mortise-and-tenon construction as other Colonial buildings, but the baroque details—the broken pediments, the pulpit, the hand-carved balustrade near the altar—speak of a more sophisticated sensibility. In a world before construction cranes, the steeple was erected in a most logical way—as a series of boxes that grow smaller as the steeple climbs higher. The bottom box of the tower functioned as a workroom for constructing the next box above it. Once built, the second box was hoisted into place on top of the first, and so on up, much the same way one section of a telescope opens out of another.

The wine-glass pulpit of Trinity Church, with the baroque sounding board above, is as elegant a piece as the Colonial world produced. Far from being purely decorative, the sounding board is a necessary part of the pulpit. A pastor of Trinity once had the sounding board removed because he found it overbearing. He was not heard by the congregation the following Sunday, and the board was restored to its original position.

Trinity's pulpit is in the center of the main aisle. In Colonial days, the sermon, not the sacraments, was the most important part of the church service. In the seventeenth-century Protestant church, Holy Communion was celebrated only twice a year, on Christmas and Easter. The weekly sermon was sometimes two hours long.

the colony house

The Colony House (Washington Square) is also a Richard Munday design. Just a few doors down from the Wanton-Lyman-Hazard House, it is a fine example of architectural sophistication during the Colonial period. Begun in 1739, the Colony House is reminiscent of a Dutch town hall, but its style and craftsmanship are typical of Munday.

The bricks that make up the Colony House probably came by ship from Bristol or Boston; they were certainly not local. (Stories say that they were once ballast in ships arriving from the Carolinas.) What is certain, is that they are smaller than the bricks of today, but have proven durable. The wooden columns supporting the ceiling inside the main room on the first floor are cased in wood, the result of a later renovation. Originally, the columns resembled the masts of ships, bare and cylindrical. The scarred floor recalls British horses that, tradition has it, were stabled here during the American Revolution.

The Colony House is steeped in history; it has housed a small brewery in its cellar, and a great many important events within its walls. Under British rule, the Colony House served as barracks for the king's troops. The English mounted a small cannon at the front door to cover the public square. In 1776, the Declaration of Independence was read from its steps by Major John Handy. George Washington, Benjamin Franklin, and other leaders of our young country walked within its halls. After the liberation of Newport from the British, the

The Colony House, 1739–44, Richard Munday, Washington Square

building became a hospital for the French, and it was here that Newport's first Catholic Mass was celebrated. Finally, when the Revolution ended, the Colony House served as a seat of the new government: It was one of five colony houses (one in each county) through which the legislative and judiciary activities rotated from the mid-eighteenth to the mid-nineteenth century. Newport and Providence were preeminent locations for these sessions.

The Redwood Library, 1748–50, Peter Harrison, Bellevue Avenue

colonial architect peter harrison

One of Newport's first professionally trained architects, Peter Harrison was born in 1716. He came to the Colonies as a young man uncertain whether to make his fortune in architecture or at sea. He was engaged as mate on a coastal ship commanded by his older brother, Joseph. At ports along the way, including some as far south as Charleston, he picked up architectural commissions. Some of Harrison's most important commissions, however, were in Newport, Rhode Island.

The Redwood Library (50 Bellevue Avenue), built in 1748, is a remarkable building for its time. It is a sophisticated English Colonial building, and a reflection that the lag time (at least in terms of building styles) between England and her American colony was narrowing. Harrison chose its design from Italy's famed Renaissance architect, Andrea Palladio—an approach that was then the height of fashion in England. Essentially a temple in the Roman Doric order, Harrison's shapely design has stood the test of time.

Harrison designed Redwood for a group dedicated to philosophical discussions (Abraham Redwood was a leading member) and it remains a private library to this day. Although the exterior is wood, the boards for the building were angle-cut to resemble blocks of stone. To enhance this illusion, Harrison mixed sand with the paint to produce a texture that looked and felt like masonry.

Peter Harrison also designed the Brick Market (Thames Street at Washington Square), in 1762, for the proprietors of Long Wharf. It served as a counting house and general market for the wharf, which had become the commercial heart of the city. Here, again, the architect used a style finely tuned in England. The Brick Market is designed after a plan developed by Inigo Jones for Somerset House in London. The building is a fine combination of classical proportions and details that lent a cosmopolitan air to Newport.

The Touro Synagogue, 1759–63, Peter Harrison, Touro Street

The Touro Synagogue (84 Touro Street), the oldest surviving synagogue in America, is another famed Harrison design. This time, there was no obvious plan for the architect to adapt, as he was not familiar with other synagogue designs. The pattern for its columns and balustrades may have come from James Gibb's book *Rules for Drawing* (circa 1700), while its two-story galleried hall closely resembles traditional Sephardic synagogues. This is not surprising, since Harrison arrived at the design only after a long series of discussions with local Jewish citizens. The resultant building is a masterpiece of simplicity and dignity. The synagogue is set at a slight angle to Touro Street in order to face the cardinal points of the compass. An entryway with classical columns is the only adornment on the otherwise cube-based design. Inside, twelve great Corinthian columns symbolizing the twelve tribes of Israel support a gallery.

The Brick Market, 1762–1772, Peter Harrison, Thames Street

These are the architect's best-known buildings, and aside from the Harrison farmhouse, (which still stands, although it has been completely altered and moved from its original site) four other houses in Newport are thought to be Harrison's. One is the Vernon House on Clarke Street, whose wooden walls are boards cut to resemble stone, as on the Redwood Library. Another, the Malbone House on Thames Street, was the brick home of one of Newport's great merchants. Additional houses thought to be Harrison's are the much-altered Peter Bulloid House at 29 Touro Street (known later as the Oliver Hazard Perry House), and the now-demolished Charles Dudley House in Middletown.

the american revolution

Newport was home to some of the precipitators of the American Revolution. There are many events worth relating, but one of the more famous concerns the dismantling of Fort George. In December of 1774, the provincial government of Newport became concerned for the safety of military stores kept at the fort. The presence of numerous warships in Newport's harbor raised concerns the British might force the colony to rebellion by seizing their ammunition, cannon, and stores. Thus, Governor Wanton and the provincial body resolved to remove all stores to the town of Providence. Historians feel the defiant dismantling of Fort George may well have given rebellious subjects of England in other parts of the Colonies renewed resolve, and inspired them to follow a similar path.

The Revolutionary War changed Newport for the moment and forever. British troops occupied Aquidneck Island from 1776 to 1779, putting an abrupt end to Newport's lucrative sea trade. The British coveted Newport and its deep-water harbor as a naval base from which to blockade patriot shipping. The British presence drove most residents from the town. During the occupation, a great many of the houses were destroyed—razed for firewood by British and colonists alike.

Within the first year of the British presence, forts were built around Aquidneck Island by the occupying forces. At the northern end, Fort Butt commanded upper Narragansett Bay. The city of Newport proper, together with the high land near the town on the western side of the island, was the seat of British power. Here, a redoubt was built to guard Easton's Beach, and another small fort was erected at Green End. The latter's earthworks can still be seen at the end of Vernon Avenue.

Blaskowitz map of Newport and Narragansett Bay, 1777, courtesy of the Newport Historical Society

BAY of NARRAGANSET in the Province of NEW ENGLAND,
with all the ISLES contained therein, among which
RHODE ISLAND and CONNONICUT
have been particularly SURVEYED.

Shewing the true position & bearings of the Banks, Shoals, Rocks &c. as likewise the Soundings.
To which have been added, the several Works & Batteries raised by the Americans.
Taken by Order of the PRINCIPAL FARMERS on Rhode Island.

By CHARLES BLASKOWITZ.

Engraved & Printed for Wm. FADEN, Charing Cross, as the Act directs July 22d 1777.

SCALE of Statute Miles

B. Pappasquash Battery
CC. Bristol Ferry Batteries
DD. Howlands Ferry Batteries
E. Goats Island Fort
F. Deere Point Battery
G. Dumpling Rocks Battery
M. Bristol Battery

A List of the Principal Farmers on
RHODE ISLAND

Mr John Gilles
Mr Isaac Brown
Mr Gabriel Bernon
Mr Benjamin Brenton
Mr Harrison
Mr Charles Wickham
Mr Church
Mr Jonathan Easton
Mr Nicholas Easton
Mr Walter Easton
Mr Esther Lawton
Mr Barker
Mr Legee
Mr Lloyd
Mr Bowler

Mr Lott
Mr Isaac Lawton
Mr Abraham Redwood
Mr Jarrat Potter
Mr Owens
Mr Ogren
Mr Rome
Mr Gould
Mr Polts phart
Mr Thomas Banister
Mr William Redwood
Mr John Banister
Mr Dudley
Mr Mallone
Mr Penn
Mr Lyons & Mr Freeman

A. White Hall with a Farm the gift of the Revd Dr Berkeley to Yale College
B. Charity Farm the Donation of John Clarke Esqr for the Relief of the Poor and bringing up Children in our Learning

PROVIDENCE RIVER

PROVIDENCE
BAY

MOUNT HOPE
BAY

BRISTOL
BAY

HOG
ISLAND

PRUDENCE

ISLAND

HOPE ISLAND

CONNONICUT
ISLAND

DUTCH ISLAND

RHODE

ISLAND

Dighton

SEAKONK RIVER

TAUNTON RIVER

Citizens of Rhode Island and General Washington wanted to see the English removed from Newport. By the second year of the British occupation, an unsuccessful attempt had been made to drive them out. General John Sullivan was then appointed supreme commander of the Rhode Island campaign, and hopes ran high that the British would be defeated during a second attempt. But a severe coastal storm prevented success. Had the weather cooperated, the war might have ended in Newport, rather than at Yorktown.

General Sullivan commanded some ten thousand Colonial troops and was supported by Count d'Estaing of France, whose fleet held tight control of Narragansett Bay, and Count de Lafayette, who headed a number of French troops. When the British heard of Sullivan's arrival nearby, they abandoned Fort Butt and consolidated their force at the southern end of the island. Sullivan immediately occupied the abandoned fort in Portsmouth. He planned to advance south and, coordinating his movements with those of the French fleet, drive the British into the sea.

Fighting with General Sullivan was a black regiment of freemen and slaves numbering over two hundred. Their actions in combat against the Hessians at the brook called Bloody Run in Portsmouth were heroic and strategically

Major General John Sullivan, courtesy of Concord Historical Society

important. Unfortunately, events that followed were both unexpected and disheartening for Sullivan and the Americans. The morning of August 12, 1778, dawned with Lord Howe's fleet abreast of Point Judith and on its way to Newport, bringing British reinforcements. D'Estaing immediately put out to sea to engage him. As he approached Howe, a great storm struck and heavily damaged both combatants who became fully engaged in spite of the ferocity of the elements. It seems that the storm did more damage than either could inflict upon the other. Several ships were dismasted, and after the engagement ended, d'Estaing withdrew to Boston for repairs. He left Sullivan poised with only a land force to accomplish the formidable task of routing the British regulars, who were well entrenched. To make matters worse, Sullivan's troops began deserting when they heard of Howe's position and d'Estaing's disappearance.

The American forces effected an orderly retreat that was brilliantly accomplished under the skillful management of Sullivan. The withdrawal took place under the cover of night, by way of Howland's Ferry at the northern end of the island, with the use of barges especially constructed for the purpose. Not one man, nor even the smallest article of equipment, was lost.

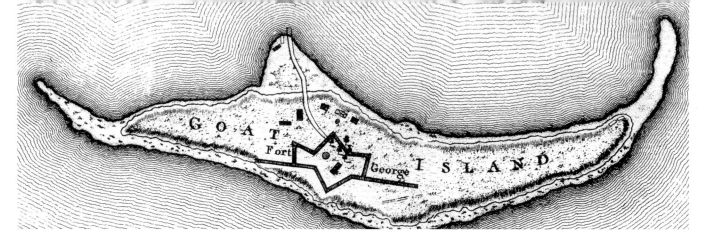

Goat Island, 1777

goat island

Goat Island, the small island that extends across Newport harbor, protecting it from raging weather, also housed a fort during the Revolution—and an extensive torpedo-manufacturing complex during World Wars I and II.

Goat Island had some of the earliest fortifications built for Newport. In the 1660s, earthworks were thrown up as a defense against the possibility of an attack by the Dutch, who were then at war with the British. The subsequent fort was designed by Peter Harrison, and the name of the fort itself changed from Fort Anne (1702–1730) to Fort George (1730–1776) to Fort Liberty (1776–1784) to Fort Washington (1784–1798) and, finally, to Fort Walcott, until it was destroyed to make way for the torpedo station in 1869.

At peak production, during WWI, thirteen thousand people commuted to work on the island by ferryboat, because the causeway bridge had not yet been built. The southern part of the island had been designated in the mid-1800s as officers' quarters for the U.S. Navy, which oversaw the operation. Houses for naval families were small, mansard-roofed

quarters, designed by James Fludder in 1871. The administration building was built on part of the foundation of Fort Wolcott. It was an impressive sight, with walls 3 feet thick. Almost one hundred years later, the naval buildings, including the administration building, were set afire to ready the island for redevelopment. The old entrenchments were still visible right up until 1972, when they were bulldozed to make way for a more modern Goat Island.

Officer's house (since razed), James Fludder, 1871, Goat Island

The Revolutionary War marked the end of the Colonial period. Perhaps the one bright spot during these rather forlorn times was the French arrival in Newport, after the British had evacuated the city, in 1780. Vernon House, possibly designed by Peter Harrison in the 1750s, served as headquarters for Comte Jean Baptiste Donatien de Vimeur Rochambeau during his stay in Newport. Exquisite craftsmanship, especially in the staircase, is unusual for a Colonial house.

Vernon House hosted a particularly famous party. The French officers, together with General George Washington, his officers, and the townspeople, celebrated the liberation of Newport in a temporary pavilion built on the northern side of the house. Newport householders dug up silver they had buried in backyards to hide it from the British. They opened their houses to their liberators and enjoyed themselves in a manner not seen during the occupation years.

Washington is said to have danced with Miss Peggy Champlin, a beauty of her day. Newporters, and especially the Champlin family, have never forgotten it. The temporary building that was set up for the dance is long gone, but Vernon House, restored in the early 1990s, is in fine repair.

The Vernon House, 1759, Peter Harrison, Clarke Street

3

the new republic takes root

Newport was crushed by the British occupation from 1776 to 1779, and little development occurred for almost sixty years. Among that development was Fort Adams, a national response to the War of 1812; a couple of mills; a church or two; and a few houses. Little happened, and not much of great consequence, especially given the burgeoning activity in almost every other place. Indeed, Newport, of all major centers of population, fell into a desuetude incomparable among its peers.

Thomas Jefferson's Monticello

St. Paul's United Methodist Church, 1806, 12 Marlborough Street

America's adoption of Classical forms was as romantic as it was intellectual. New public buildings had a high purpose—to house offices of The New Republic. It was quite reasonable to choose ancient Roman structures as models. Roman government and laws had stood the test of centuries and had an appealing vastness and inherent dignity.

A private house was a different matter. While Thomas Jefferson's home, Monticello, in Charlottesville, Virginia, used a Roman format successfully, more often it proved awkward to reduce Roman forms to private dwellings. Details from large Roman public structures lost their dignity when translated onto the smaller American house. Classical Greek architecture supplied a solution (as, indeed, it had in the early years of the eighteenth century, and in Western Europe before that): its clean lines strongly influenced residential construction in the second quarter of the nineteenth century.

Though Newport faced a particularly long road ahead in terms of its development, its patriotic pride swelled when America was finally liberated from the British. The former colonists, now citizens of the United States of America, sought a new style of architecture both to dignify their public buildings and to signify a new, national identity. The Federal style, which arose after the Revolution and flourished into the early nineteenth century, has its basis in Neoclassicism, a style that was sweeping Europe at the same time. In its American manifestation, as elsewhere, it combined elements of ancient Greek and Roman architecture.

Pattern book illustration by Asher Benjamin

The Whitehorne Museum, 420 Thames Street

The Robert Lawton House, 1809, 118 Mill Street

Saint Paul's Church is a fine example of Federal-style architecture. Built in 1806, Saint Paul's is Colonial in scale, but sports a Palladian window and has a small dome topping its steeple. Its design was documented in a pattern book by Asher Benjamin in the early 1800s (shown on page 41) although it is not clear whether Benjamin's drawing inspired the church's design, or vice versa.

The Whitehorne Museum at 420 Thames Street (now restored) and the Robert Lawton House at 118 Mill Street, are further examples of the Federal style in Newport. Like the Lawton House, the Whitehorne House (1811, now the Whitehorne Museum) shows the straightforward, square shape of the Federal style, with an abundance of refined detail. Built by Capt. Samuel Whitehorne in the early 1800s, it was impressive, though not ostentatious, for its time. The young captain had four ships plying the waters, which promised rich rewards. Unfortunately, he lost two ships at sea, and even though he was involved in a great many other enterprises, including a bank, an iron foundry, and a distillery, he never recovered financially and his house was sold at auction in 1844. The fine doorway with fanlight and columns makes a stately entrance. Inside, there are rooms on either side of the entrance hall, with an impressive arch spanning the passage. At the back of the hall is a graceful stairway. The bull's-eye window in the façade also marks the Whitehorne home as a Federal house.

The Greek Revival period in the early nineteenth century reflected a hierarchical, formal plan. The Greek temple was adopted as a model partly for political reasons: Greece had been the cradle of democracy, and Americans had fought a war in order to give birth to democracy in the Western Hemisphere. The high ideals and noble forms of the ancient Greeks were just being discovered and brought back to England by archeologists. Meanwhile, Greece was fighting a war for independence against the Turks. This became something of a cause célèbre for the rest of the world—a symbol of democracy's emergence from tyranny. Knowledge of Grecian architecture and ideals became a status symbol. It was considered scholarly to study Greek (especially ancient Greek); to know the details of Greek architecture was important for the wealthy and ambitious.

In this context, it is easy to understand why the song "My Country 'Tis of Thee" praises "thy rocks and rills and templed hills." The hills of the United States were literally templed with little classical buildings from 1800 to 1830.

Elmhyrst, 1833–1835, Warren and Bucklin, One Mile Corner, Middletown

Houses with Greek Revival influence, circa 1876,
from *The Newport Atlas of 1876*

the greek revival house

Although the Greek Revival period was not the first time
popular architecture showed a formal, rigid symmetry, a high
concentration of Greek Revival houses still stands in the area
between John and Mill streets. This portion of a map from
The Newport Atlas of 1876 shows this area, bordered by
Bellevue Avenue to the east and Spring Street to the west.
The structures in red are Greek-influenced.

The typical Greek Revival house consists of a simple, rectangular floor plan with a central hall. Usually, there are two rooms on each side of the hall, with a stairway at the end of the hall leading to a second floor. The stairway afforded an opportunity for refinement and a certain degree of originality.

Variations of the plan were dictated by the size of the house. Sometimes, the central hall was placed to one side, and the first floor comprised only two rooms. In general, however, the Greek Revival style was conforming, symmetrical, and uncompromising.

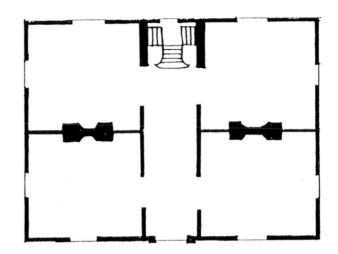

Typical Greek Revival floor plan

THE GOLDEN MEAN

The ratio of the lengths of *A* to *B* is the same as the ratio of *B* to *A+B*. This is the so-called golden mean that was at the heart of all Greek design. This mathematical universal was used throughout the Greek Revival period, as it was in Greece, and indeed it is such a strong design concept that it permeates design in Western society, even now. Overall window shapes and formats for rectangular structures of all sorts usually can be traced to this shape.

These ratios were used in all aspects of the houses of the 1820s and 1830s. The harmony of proportions in the Greek Revival house lends dignity to the structure, as well as a gracefulness that sets it apart from the rest of the houses in town.

Proportions

The Golden Rectangle

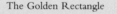

The Golden Rectangle can be constructed this way:

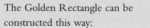

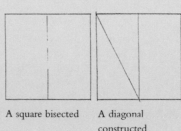 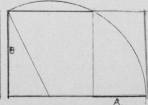

A square bisected   A diagonal constructed at the bisection   The diagonal used as the radius and scribed to intersect the base extended

The Golden Mean
A:B as *B:A+B* is the so-called golden mean that was the heart of all Greek design.

Postcard of the Original Placement of the Elmhyrst Buildings,
Courtesy of Mr. Robert Elder

growing prosperity

After the War of 1812, trade with the East began flourishing again in Newport, as elsewhere in New England. Whereas the Hunter House on Washington Street (see page 29) is a prime example of a Colonial sea captain's home, a brilliant nineteenth-century variation on the same theme is Elmhyrst (One Mile Corner), built by the Vernon family in 1835.

The Vernons also owned a house on Clarke Street thought to have been designed by Peter Harrison in the 1750s for Metcalf Bowler. This became famous in its own right as Rochambeau's headquarters during the Revolutionary War. The family built Elmhyrst as a country house. It was designed by the firm of Warren, Tallman & Bucklin.

Elmhyrst is one of the best examples of the Greek Revival in Newport. Three buildings occupy the site; each is a stylistic variation. The main house, illustrated in color here, is elegant with its Ionic columns. In its refined Corinthian style, the library, just to the south, reflects the Vernon family's reverence for learning. A little outbuilding, possibly the gardener's cottage, is simple, utilitarian Doric in style.

Elmhyrst, 1833–1835, Warren, Tallman & Bucklin

The Swinburne School, 115 Pelham Street

Photo courtesy of the Newport Historical Society

The house at 115 Pelham Street, also Greek Revival (used as the Swinburne School), is one of three along that street once belonging to mariners. Like the Vernon family, many of the seamen on Pelham Street were involved in the tea trade. This house, built in the mid-1800s, stands on land that belonged to Governor Benedict Arnold in the 1600s.

An example of a public building remodeled in Greek Revival style during the early nineteenth century is the Second Congregational Church on Clarke Street. Its diminutive, makeshift spire was erected in 1846; the original (seen in the photograph) was dismantled after a damaging hurricane.

Opposite: Second Congregational Church, Clarke Street, Cotton Palmer

The main body of the church sports all the accoutrements of the Greek Revival. The corner pilasters are constructed in a framework of wood, symbolizing simple columns. This translation to wood of the Greek style can be found in many Newport buildings. However, the era of the Greek Revival house was short-lived in Newport. It marked a time of intellectual optimism that sought a simple expression in architecture. Great changes lay just ahead.

newport in transition: at work and play

By the mid-1800s, a new era was dawning. The Industrial Revolution was a threat as well as a promise, and both were felt in Newport. While it never became an industrial city, Newport did see a rise in manufacturing. Meanwhile, the smoke, squalor, and noise of other more industrialized cities made the pristine beaches of Aquidneck Island more attractive. Travel became easier during the age of canal boats, railroads, and steamers. And the wealthy began vacationing in Newport.

Newport waterfront, Washington Street

Newport waterfront in the 1800s, courtesy of the Newport Historical Society

The Perry Mill, 1835, Alexander MacGregor, corner of Thames Street and America's Cup Boulevard

the mills and the forts

With the coming of the Industrial Revolution, New Bedford, Massachusetts, became the capital of whaling on the New England mainland, while shipbuilding was centered in Bristol, Rhode Island. (Neither trade had managed to catch on as strongly in Newport, although the town had been an important manufacturer of spermacetti candles and a great center for privateers prior to the American Revolution.) Meanwhile, textiles had their day in Newport.

Newport architect John Grosvenor writes:

In 1835, Alexander MacGregor, a Scottish stone-mason and architect, built the Perry Mill, one of two textile mills still remaining from Newport's industrial period. Built to manufacture delaine, a light woolen dress fabric, Perry specialized in cotton prints after

1850. At its peak in 1878, it employed about 150 workers, but by the turn of the century it was out of business. It found subsequent use as a roller rink, a bowling alley and, in World War II, as housing for workers at the torpedo station on Goat Island.

The original stone structure rose four stories and had a steeply gabled roof, a full-length clerestory, and a Greek Revival belfry. The Perry Mill and the Aquidneck Mill, which was also established in the 1830s, were built with high hopes and great expectations, but Newport never developed a significant industrial base.

The Perry Mill's steeply gabled roof and tower, lost after years of neglect and three hurricanes, were restored in 1982 by the Newport Collaborative Architects, Inc., to support the mill's current use as a hotel and time-share condominiums.

A few other nineteenth-century commercial enterprises did somewhat better in Newport. There were breweries (one located, logically, on Brewer Street) and several distilleries. The tower of a lead-shot factory stood high on the skyline at the Brown and Howard Wharf, a few hundred yards north of the Wellington Avenue intersection. It is quite visible in the 1873 illustration on this page.

Fort Adams, Eastern Wall

FORT ADAMS

Due to Newport's strategic location at the entrance to Narragansett Bay, military developments have had more impact on the city than manufacturing. Early forts existed on Goat Island (see Chapter 2), Rose Island, and at the point of land where Fort Adams was subsequently built (started in 1824, it was completed in the early 1850s.) This massive installation was built on the site of a previous fortification (though not much is known about the earlier fort, save that it shows up on some Revolutionary War maps.) It assumed its present form a little more than a quarter of a century after the Revolution, and never saw wartime action.

Newport skyline, *Harper's Weekly*, August 30, 1873

Fort Adams, view from the north

Fort Adams is important for several reasons. First, of course, it protected Newport and the bay. Second, it introduced a new aesthetic to the city, that of stone construction. As the nineteenth century developed, stone made a new, forceful statement throughout Newport. Third, the construction of Fort Adams coincided with an influx of Irish immigrants, who were brought over for their stonebuilding skills and stayed to help build some of Newport's more massive nineteenth-century buildings.

Fort Adams was planned as part of a national system of coastal fortifications, established by Congress, following the country's invasion during the War of 1812. A military architect, Colonel Joseph Totten, designed it, while Major Toussard oversaw construction. French military engineer Simon Bernard's design for the fort followed in the tradition of Vauban, a great French military designer. These, in turn, harked back to the star-shaped Renaissance forts of Filarete and Martini. Alexander

MacGregor, the stonemason who would build Perry Mill eleven years later, set to work on Fort Adams in 1824 (he was the construction engineer on the project).

This bastion represented the state of the fort-builder's art in the nineteenth century. To guard against an attack by land from the south, a narrow, low-lying corridor ran along the southern wall, with a small gate opening to the west. In effect, this acted like a moat. Inside the moat were wedge-shape islands, strategically placed to divide an invading force. This area was covered by gun slits in the walls and cannon emplacements at salient points. In addition, the interior casement batteries—aimed at the harbor entrance, with land fortifications just behind—consisted of guns mounted in pairs, housed in domed chambers, and running the length of the walls. Such overwhelming defenses, concentrated in one place, easily controlled the narrow approach between Jamestown and Newport, all the way to the upper bay and Providence.

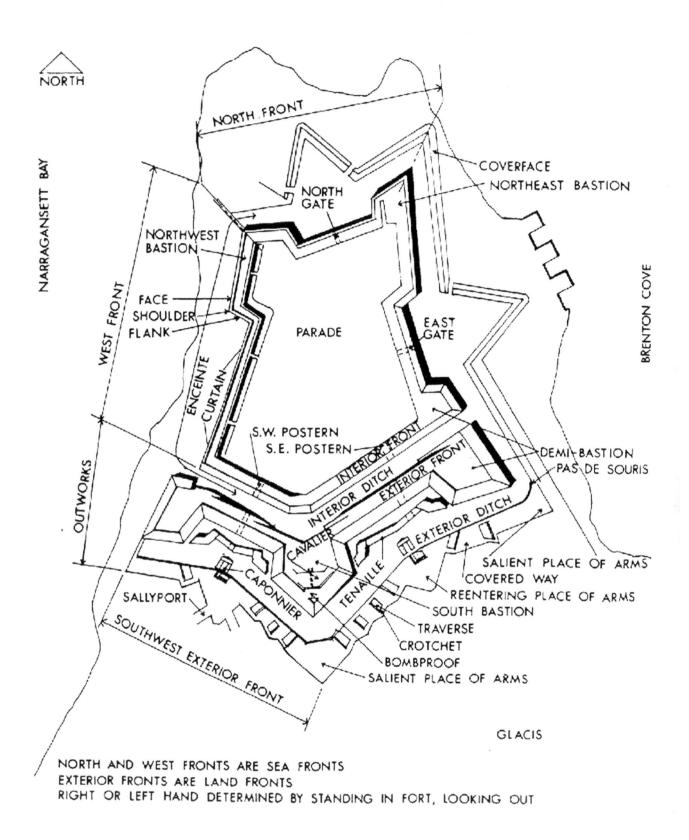

NORTH

NARRAGANSETT BAY

NORTH FRONT

COVERFACE
NORTHEAST BASTION

NORTH GATE

NORTHWEST BASTION

WEST FRONT

FACE
SHOULDER
FLANK

PARADE

EAST GATE

ENCEINTE
CURTAIN

BRENTON COVE

OUTWORKS

S.W. POSTERN
S.E. POSTERN

INTERIOR FRONT
INTERIOR DITCH
EXTERIOR FRONT

DEMI-BASTION
PAS DE SOURIS

CAVALIER

EXTERIOR DITCH

SALLYPORT

CAPONNIER

TENAILLE

EXTERIOR DITCH

SALIENT PLACE OF ARMS
COVERED WAY
REENTERING PLACE OF ARMS
SOUTH BASTION
TRAVERSE
CROTCHET
BOMBPROOF
SALIENT PLACE OF ARMS

SOUTHWEST EXTERIOR FRONT

GLACIS

NORTH AND WEST FRONTS ARE SEA FRONTS
EXTERIOR FRONTS ARE LAND FRONTS
RIGHT OR LEFT HAND DETERMINED BY STANDING IN FORT, LOOKING OUT

Fairmere
Newport R.I.

Richard Grosv
Feb

stone buildings

Before the nineteenth century, stone did not play a major role in Newport construction. Although the Old Stone Mill is Newport's first known structure, wood otherwise was the building material of choice, in part because wood was plentiful, in part because Newporters were accustomed to working with wood in shipbuilding.

The influx of Irish stone workers brought a new dimension to the city. Hired to work on the construction of Fort Adams, the Irish settled first in the Kerry Hill area, near Kingston Avenue. Shortly afterward, in order to be closer both to Fort Adams and to the quarries off Ruggles Avenue and Wickham Road, many moved south to lower Thames Street, thus forming the so-called Fifth Ward (actually the ethnically Irish part of the Fourth Ward). Newport's quarries yielded a fine, brown granite used first by MacGregor, and then by others.

Catholicism arrived with the Irish. The first Catholic church, built in 1840s, was located on Barney Street; a few years later, the Fort Adams builders used their skills to construct St. Mary's Church on Spring Street. In 1853, this handsome brownstone church dominated the Newport skyline. Another faith had joined the city that has stood for religious freedom since its founding.

Above: St. Mary's Church, 1848–52, Patrick Keeley, Spring Street and Memorial Boulevard

Opposite: Lansmere, 1852–53, Alexander MacGregor, Webster Street

Halidon Hall, Alexander MacGregor, Harborview Drive

alexander macgregor

Alexander MacGregor (1796–1870) is recognized as a master stonemason but his contributions to the Newport scene rank him as an architect as well. The monumental scale of Mac-Gregor's work is impressively bold.

Having built public structures such as the Perry Mill and Fort Adams earlier in his career, he later turned his talent in the 1850s to designing summer residences.

Swanhurst, 1851, Alexander MacGregor, Bellevue Avenue and Webster Street

Swanhurst at Bellevue Avenue and Webster Street is an Italianate home of stucco over granite. Swanhurst, Lansmere (72 Webster Street), and Stoneleigh (61 Narragansett Avenue)—which form a distinct neighborhood—are characteristic of a generation of pre–Civil War summer homes. Each has a boldly massed two-story stone exterior, accompanying outbuildings, and a circular drive. These country villas were sited to take advantage of a westward expanse over meadows and marshlands to Newport's harbor, views now obstructed by other buildings. At the time of his death in June, 1870, Alexander MacGregor left a legacy of granite as part of Newport's cityscape. As architect John Grosvenor notes, by the very nature of the material and the quality of MacGregor's craft, these may endure for centuries.

Kingscote, 1839–41, Richard Upjohn,
253 Bellevue Avenue and East Bowery Street

summer visitors

There were good reasons for the wealthy to summer in Newport—the climate, the glorious vistas, and the company of one's peers. During the 1840s, Newport became a resort for the well-to-do, and Aquidneck Island became a sporting place. Initially, the favorite pastime was public bathing, which had just come to the fore, especially at hotels overlooking magnificent beaches. Tennis and fox hunting came next, and yachting followed shortly after.

Prior to the Civil War, there were many Southerners among the summer gentry of Aquidneck Island. They flocked to the North to escape unbearable heat. The war created a dilemma for them, however, as they suddenly found themselves unwelcome in Newport, or anywhere else north of the Mason-Dixon Line. The Noble Jones family was one of those who sadly decided to leave the house they had built for themselves only a little more than a decade before. When the King family bought it, they changed its name to Kingscote (253 Bellevue Avenue).

One of the most visible signs of the Civil War in Newport was the conversion of the Atlantic House on Pelham Street to the U.S. Naval Academy. Located at the corner of Bellevue Avenue and Pelham Street, the academy housed midshipmen during the Civil War. When the building was destroyed shortly after the war, the Academy moved back to Annapolis, Maryland.

Many women of Newport were involved in the war in one way or another. Julia Ward Howe—famous for her 1862 song "The Battle Hymn of the Republic," which inspired the Union Army as it marched to war—lived in the "Kay–Catherine" area.

Katherine Prescott Wormeley lived on Red Cross Avenue in 1876. An eminent scholar and translator, she had worked with the U.S. Sanitary Commission (a precursor of the American Red Cross) during the Civil War. Ms. Wormeley worked on the commission's hospital ships dispatched to coastal waters off Virginia to receive and care for the wounded.

The Atlantic House, Pelham Street and Bellevue Avenue, destroyed in the 1870s

Ocean House, courtesy of the Newport Historical Society

newport hotels

The Newport hotel had its heyday in the mid-nineteenth century. Passenger ships and pleasure craft from New York plied Long Island Sound past Fisher's Island to Newport. Visitors disembarked at the end of Long Wharf, whence they were transported by carriage to their hotels. A rail connection from Boston to Fall River meant the advent of Bostonians, as well.

By 1859, there were five hotels of significance in Newport: the Ocean House, rebuilt by Russell Warren after the fire of 1845, in Gothic style, with a double tier of porches; the

The Ocean House, 1845, Russell Warren & Son,
Bellevue Avenue and East Bowery

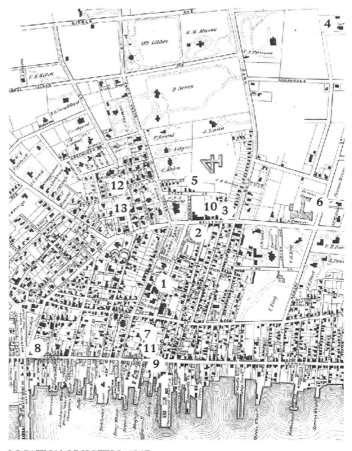

LOCATION OF HOTELS, 1867

1. AQUIDNECK HOUSE, PELHAM/CORNE
2. ATLANTIC HOUSE, PELHAM/BELLEVUE
3. CLARENDON HOTEL, DEBLOIS/BELLEVUE
4. CLIFF HOUSE, DRESSER ST.
5. GERMANIA HOUSE, LIBERTY AT DOWNING
6. OCEAN HOUSE, BELLEVUE/EAST BOWERY
7. PELHAM ST. HOUSE, 12 PELHAM ST.
8. PERRY HOUSE, WASH. SQ./THAMES
9. STEAMBOAT HOTEL, 209 THAMES
10. TOURO HOUSE, 140 BELLEVUE AVE.
11. U.S. HOTEL, PELHAM/THAMES
12. FILMORE, CATHERINE ST.
13. BELLEVUE HOUSE, CATHERINE ST.

Location of hotels, 1867

Atlantic House built in Classical style in 1844; the United States Hotel; the Fillmore; and the Bellevue House. In addition, the Seaview House (built sometime after 1870), which burned down in the first part of the twentieth century, was built on Cliff Avenue. Some of the cottages from this complex are still extant near the cliffs in that area.

With public bathing a new and popular pastime, the long strand of Easton's Beach drew droves of summer visitors. Close to the heart of town, it could be reached easily, either by walking or, after the 1870s, by streetcar. Newport had an active night life, as well. All summer long, hotels offered dance music—most of it by German bands hired for the season. It was the era of waltzes and polkas.

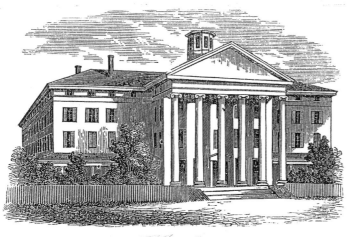

ATLANTIC HOUSE.

Atlantic House, 1840–44, courtesy of the Newport Historical Society

The Newport Daily News described the dancing and the music:

> At the hotels, particularly at the "Ocean" (House),
> they commenced dancing immediately after breakfast,
> and it was continued until a late hour of the night,
> with but slight interruptions for bathing, etc. Since
> then, the dancing has decreased, until the present sea-
> son, when there is comparatively little. This season,
> the visitors amuse themselves by dancing a little, talk-
> ing a great deal, walking, listening to the Germania
> music at the houses, attending their concerts, prome-
> nading at the hotels, gathering in little companies and
> conversing pleasantly. (August 13, 1851)

A decade later, English novelist Anthony Trollope sniffed at American excess:

> In England we knew nothing of hotels prepared for
> six hundred visitors, all of whom are expected to live
> in common. Domestic architects would be frightened
> by the dimensions which are needed, and at the
> number of apartments which are required to be clus-
> tered under one roof. We went to the Ocean House
> at Newport, and fancied, as we first entered the hall
> under a verandah as high as the house, and made
> our way into the passage, that we had taken to be a
> well-arranged barrack. (From North America,
> Harper Brothers, New York, 1862).

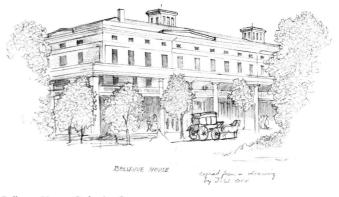

BELLEVUE HOUSE

copied from a drawing by J. W. Orr

Bellevue House, Catherine Street

Two of the hotels, the Bellevue and the Fillmore, were built in the Kay–Catherine–Old Beach Road area. It was only a matter of time before the land behind these hotels was developed. Alfred Smith and Joseph Bailey started selling lots in this part of town in 1860, and the area attracted a wealth of interesting summer residents. The cultured group that George Champlin Mason urged to come from Philadelphia, New York, Harvard, and M.I.T. included the Boston essayist and poet Thomas Gold Appleton, singer Charlotte Cushman, and architect, artist, and M.I.T. founder William Barton Rogers.

After the Old Beach Road area was well under way, developers Bailey and Smith turned their attention to the southern end of the island, the location that would become Bellevue Avenue. The building of Bellevue Avenue was perhaps the single most important event influencing the demise of the era of hotels. With Bellevue came the new era of "the cottages."

For many years the area sloping toward Easton's Beach had been orchards and farm fields. Old Beach Road leading to the beach from Bellevue Avenue (then Touro Street) was treacherous; there were two right-angle corners on the way down. Young drivers trying to impress their female companions by racing to the beach had, on occasion, tipped over their rigs when they came to the marker (still in place) at the corner of Old Beach Road and Rhode Island Avenue (then called Love's Lane). The next corner, that of Love's Lane and Bath Road, was just as challenging for very much the same reason.

Bellevue Avenue

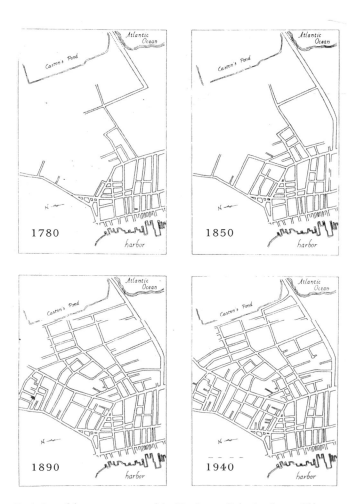

Evolution of the street pattern of the Kay Street, Catherine Street, Old Beach Road neighborhood

newport in transition: at home

The second half of the nineteenth century witnessed a profileration of domestic styles of organic architecture—the Cottage Ornée, the Swiss Chalet, and the Stick, Italianate, Queen Anne, and Shingle styles. All part of the Victorian era, this was an age of experimentation and growth, and Newport became a showplace of ideas.

Thomas Cushing House, 1876, George Champlin Mason
(no longer standing)

the organic house

The Organic House was a reaction to the restraints imposed by the symmetry and rigidity of classical design that had held sway since the Renaissance. After years of living within the bounds of classicicsm, mid-nineteenth century designers and clients shook off conformity to this abstract, unyielding design approach. Nooks and crannies, and a well-placed balcony overlooking an interesting view became desirable features; architecture finally began to reflect the individual preferences of those who lived in the houses.

It also reflected a growing interest in nature. The black clouds of coal smoke and noise from the mills of the Industrial Revolution spurred a reaction, both in America and in England, against everything industrial. In homebuilding, this spurred architects to better integrate their designs with natural settings. Interiors were equally affected. Woodwork was shaped and carved to echo natural forms. Flower designs wound their way into panels and mantelpieces.

William Morris led a movement back to handicrafts, and Richard Norman Shaw's architecture in England reflected a return to the Tudor style. These returns to the past and to nature were escapes from reality. Men who dreamed of King Arthur's knights and planned their houses to be reminiscent of the Arthurian Age were implying that the present was too horrible to face.

It is ironic that the same industrial growth at which they shuddered was the source of their wealth and leisure, which,

Benjamin Marsh House,
1845, School Street

Griswold House, 1862–64, Richard Morris Hunt, 76 Bellevue Avenue

in turn, enabled them to dream. It also brought technological innovations like central heating (an innovation every well-to-do Victorian family must have) and the powered scroll saw (which enabled the Victorian builder to embellish his cottages with "gingerbread").

In the mid-nineteenth century, there was also an interest in building with new materials and textures, and a rediscovery of handicrafts. John La Farge traveled to France and visited Breton churches to absorb the designs of medieval stained glass. His work blossomed into techniques used in the Congregational Church windows on Pelham Street. La Farge glass was also used in Channing Church and in Linden Gate, as well as the Marquand House designed by R.M. Hunt. Louis Comfort Tiffany, La Farge's most active competitor, developed remarkably similar glass techniques, and these two artists were involved in a rivalry most of their lives.

The artists, artisans, and architects of the period who revived an interest in materials also believed in the integrity of their use. It was important, for instance, that a house's siding express its support function. Trees grew vertically; hence, Alexander Jackson Downing reasoned that the wood should be employed vertically on houses. The house of the mid-nineteenth century began to demonstrate an "articulation" that previously had been obscured.

Samuel Pratt House, 1871–72, Bellevue Avenue

the cottage ornée

The connectedness of man and nature had been a principal theme of the eighteenth-century French philosopher Jean Jacques Rousseau. His belief in the natural goodness of man and the benefits of a life lived in contact with nature were picked up by other thinkers. These included the Englishman John Claudius Loudon, who preached a cleansing of the soul through living in an uncomplicated rural setting. In the United States, the teachings of Ralph Waldo Emerson had a great impact. He made two things clear: independence was a quality to be admired, and nature reflects the Almighty.

Such thinking influenced landscape designers such as Frederick Law Olmsted and Andrew Jackson Downing. While Olmsted rose to prominence during and after the Civil War,

Downing made his mark somewhat earlier, before his death at age thirty-seven in 1852. His book *Cottage Residences*, coauthored by Alexander Jackson Davis, was a pattern book of simple dwellings in natural settings, stripped of exotic trappings that Downing feared were not good for the soul.

Among those influenced by Davis was the architect Richard Upjohn who, in 1841, completed for George Noble Jones a so-called cottage ornée known as Kingscote (253 Bellevue Avenue).

Gothic in spirit, the cottage ornée emulated and harmonized with nature. The gingerbread under the cornice cast dappled shadows on the walls, like the shadows of trees in the forest. The siding was of wide boards, set vertically with battens. Windows were Gothic, and crenelated battlements decorated upstairs balconies. The chimney pots harked back to the Middle Ages.

Architecturally, nature could best be appreciated by letting her invade the borders of a house. As a result, the porch became an important feature of nineteenth-century homes. Earth hues became the colors of choice, replacing the white of the Greek Revival. Bright colors were sometimes used idiosyncratically to accentuate architectural details. Classic columns were replaced by vertical supports that emulated nature. Some supports were bundles of sticks, entwined in tendrils; others were of simulated bamboo. Patterns showing dahlias, daisies, and sun disks found their way onto facades

Samuel Pratt House, 1871–72, Bellevue Avenue

and even inside. Many times, decorative elements were set off-center, as strict symmetry was considered unnatural.

The Samuel Pratt House, opposite the Redwood Library on Bellevue Avenue, is vividly ornamented. The gambrel roof with struts is in keeping with the chalet style described on page 74, while the vertical siding boards reflect Downing's influence. Of interest are the floral designs on the "punch board" railings. The multifaceted slates on the wall are consistent with the Victorian love of texture. Small gargoyles sit at the corners of the gambrel roof.

The Edward King House, 1845–47, Aquidneck Park

the italianate style

While the neoclassicism of the early nineteenth century was overturned in the latter half of the century, classic styles have long remained a touchstone of stability in our culture. In our search for dignity and a cohesive link with the past, forms of the ancient world are perceived to have lasting value. So while Americans were experimenting with more natural architectural forms, the Italianate style also rose to prominence.

Modest, yet monumental, such homes seemed to reflect the taste of the Kay–Catherine–Old Beach Road area. Houses of this type usually have arched windows and heavy, overhanging eaves, supported by brackets of unusual, intricate shapes. Usually, a tower is included in the design, which anchors all the elements of the house and provides a focus for its massing. Many such houses line Kay Street. Their strong facades almost seemed sculpted.

Italianate tendencies can be found incorporated with any number of other styles in Newport. The Edward King House is a notable Italianate example in brick. This mansion was designed in 1848 by Richard Upjohn who, just ten years before, had designed the cottage ornée Kingscote. The King House is a monument to geometry yet the towers arc distinctly asymmetrical. The most recognizable Italianate characteristic is the strong use of arches.

One of the most interesting Italianate houses in Newport is Bienvenu (Narragansett Avenue), built originally for Joseph Hart of Troy, New York. E. D. Morgan bought it in 1868 and greatly expanded the house. In 1888, it was expanded again by J.D. Johnston. This house dominates its location on the street with its sheer weight and with the strength and massing of its tower.

Bienvenu, 1853-54, Narragansett Avenue

The Chalet on Halidon Hill, 1866–67, Richard Morris Hunt, Chastellux Avenue

the swiss chalet

Unadorned wood in straight sticks also had great appeal for the house builders of the third quarter of the nineteenth century. The Swiss chalet incorporated qualities much sought after by proponents of the new organic style. These houses, which had already won popular acceptance in Europe, included niceties of living that the Greek Revival houses did not. Porches adjoined rooms on both floors while windows were big, letting in lots of light. The shadows cast by the framework of sticks under the gable gave added dimension to the facade.

A number of Swiss chalet houses can be found on the streets of Newport. One of the best known is The Chalet on the hill above the Ida Lewis Yacht Club. This structure (the original core and entrance) was thought at one time to have been designed by Leopold Eidlitz, but it is now generally attributed to Richard Morris Hunt.

George Champlin Mason's chalet, on the corner of Old Beach Road and Sunnyside Place, is a masterpiece of organic decoration. The porches and the triangular punchboard decoration under the gables are resplendent with plant designs. The batten construction gives a vertical emphasis that would have pleased Andrew Jackson Downing.

TRADITION AND INNOVATION

Architects were versatile. Sometimes those who seemed to be initiating new modes would hark back to well-established styles, and vice versa. It was a great age for both tradition and invention. In 1863, John Hubbard Sturgis designed a house in the Second-Empire style for Frederick Rhinelander, at 10 Redwood Street. Other commissions included Greenvale Farm (1864–65), a Portsmouth house of great gables and gingerbread for John S. Barstow; and a full-blown stick-style house (1867) for the Robert M. Cushing family.

Frederick Rhinelander House, 1863, John Hubbard Sturgis, 10 Redwood Street

the stick style

Following close on the heels of the Swiss chalet was the stick style. The two were closely related; both highlighted and celebrated the house's wooden structure.

This style is well described by architectural historian Vincent Scully, who originated the name:

> *The visual effect is of a skinless architecture with all its nerves and tendons exposed. It is an architecture of sticks, expressing the structural fact of its frame. This quality of the stick is even more apparent in those shadowy voids which Downing loved, the piazza and the verandah.* (The Shingle Style and the Stick Style, *Yale, 1955*)

As Scully notes, the stick style was based on the theory and work of the Englishman Gervase Wheeler, who arrived in the United States in the 1840s. In *The Shingle Style and the Stick Style*, Scully quotes Wheeler:

> *The construction itself, though simple, is somewhat peculiar. It is framed, but in such a manner as that on the exterior, the construction shows and gives additional rightness and character to the composition.*
>
> *At the corners are heavy posts roughly dressed and chamfered and into them are mortised horizontal ties, immediately under the springing of the roof; these, with the posts, and the studs, and the framing of the roof, showing externally.*

The stick style arose not only from an interest in exposed-wood construction but also from a technological advance in the manufacture of nails. In the early 1800s, wire nails began to be mass-produced and their price dropped dramatically. The mortise-and-tenon joining of earlier post-and-beam construction gave way to a lighter, easier building style: the balloon frame. This was the use of two-by-four stock nailed together, instead of larger pieces laboriously fitted together, to form the frame of a house.

The Andrews House (553 Bellevue Avenue), designed by George Champlin Mason, is an example of highly developed stick style architecture. The style, initiated in Newport by Hunt and then amplified by Mason, gives an organic feel to the building. It is truly an architecture of bones and tendons. This house on Bellevue Avenue, just opposite Rosecliff, still exists today, but only as the interior framework for a much more extensive building that designed by Francis L. Hoppin, a Rhode Island–born architect who worked with the firm of McKim, Mead and White. The existing building, remodeled at the beginning of the twentieth century, is called Sherwood.

Mrs. Loring Andrews House, 1871–72, George Champlin Mason, Bellevue Avenue

William Watts Sherman House, 1875,
Henry Hobson Richardson, Shephard Avenue

the queen anne style

Around the 1880s, Americans with newly earned industrial wealth began to travel in earnest. On "the grand tour" of Europe, Americans were exposed to the chateaux of the Loire Valley and other grand European mansions. A taste for faraway places and the exotic was soon reflected in domestic architecture in the United States. The Queen Anne style lasted from the mid–1870s until well after 1900 in the United States. (Queen Anne, a Stuart queen of England, reigned from 1702 to 1714.)

The houses of this style are basically medieval in spirit, generally half-timbered, and their facades sport a great deal of texture and detail. They are the most fanciful and ebullient of all the Victorian houses. Usually, this style consists of a treasure trove of gables with textured shingles, stucco, barge boards, and raking cornices with flowered patterns. Details abound, the most important of which is inside—a "living hall" that was the very heart of the house. Replacing the parlor of former times, the hall is charged with a great feeling of space. The ceiling is high, and a staircase and fireplace are featured. Further, the living hall is a great connector of space to the rest of the rooms, and consequently its surfaces—the walls, floor, and ceiling—are lavish.

The William Watts Sherman House (35 Shepard Avenue), designed by Henry Hobson Richardson, is considered the first Queen Anne house in the country. The genius of the architect is embodied here in the texture of the facade, the warm living hall, the rich interior woodwork, and the stained glass windows that gave special light to the whole interior (sadly, those windows are now gone).

The Baldwin House (420 Bellevue Avenue) is of special note because it was restored in 2001. The same family has owned it since it was built.

Stanford White sketch of the Watts Sherman House, courtesy of the Providence Public Library

C.C. Baldwin House, 1880, George B. Post, Bellevue and Narragansett avenues

The Isaac Bell House, 1881–83,
McKim, Mead, and White,
Bellevue Avenue at Perry Street

the shingle style

The sharp edges of the stick and Queen Anne styles became rounded and more organic with the advent of the shingle style. The use of wood shingles permitted a certain flow of architectural forms; the verandah allows outside space to flow into the home.

Great shingled houses were built in Newport, especially around Kay Street. Some of these houses sported emblazoned fronts; almost always, they had curving porches and, inevitably, large chimneys. The magnificent living hall of the Queen Anne style continued, while the advent of central heating made it possible to heat these vast spaces.

The house on Bellevue Avenue at Perry Street, designed by McKim, Mead, and White, and built for Isaac Bell, has a movable oak-paneled wall on rollers to afford a flexible space inside. The exterior has an exotic tower in the shape of a bell (an allusion to the original owner's name?) along with bamboo-like spindles that hold up the wide verandah. Two dolphin-like creatures support the end of the porch roof by the front door. The shingle style is extravagant but playful.

Painstakingly restored in the 1990s by the Preservation Society of Newport County (under curator Paul Miller), the Isaac Bell House exemplifies the shingle style and is, perhaps, the high point of an architecture that claims to be American, in every sense of the word.

mason and newton, architects

George Champlin Mason and Dudley Newton were two local architects whose work had a profound effect on the fabric of Newport, especially the area downtown. Their work helped the city fully recover and move on from the devastation of the Revolutionary War era and the early nineteenth-century embargo that followed, and even today their designs are woven everywhere into the cloth of the city. George Champlin Mason worked with Alfred Smith and Joseph Bailey to help establish the Kay-Catherine-Old Beach Road area. Smith was also instrumental in having Bellevue Avenue built, as well as the Cliff Walk and Ocean Drive. Yet, the importance of Mason and Newton (who began as Mason's apprentice) is seldom acknowledged properly. As the adage has it, they were prophets unrecognized in their own country—even their own city.

W.G. Weld House, 1881, Dudley Newton, Bellevue Avenue

Heartsease, 1882, George Champlin Mason,
corner of Ayrault and Kay Streets
(For C.N. Beach of Hartford, Connecticut)

george champlin mason

Mason was born to Newport's merchant aristocracy in 1820. During his childhood and youth, the city's economy stagnated. As a young man, Mason sailed to Europe where he studied architecture and drawing for two years. When he returned home, he hoped to make his mark as a landscape painter, but he saw little financial future here. So he turned himself to the double career of real estate agent and newspaper publishing. In 1849, at the age of twenty-nine, he became an editor for the *Newport Advertiser*, also serving as a correspondent for the *Providence Journal* and the *New York Evening Post*. In 1860, he established his architectural firm.

Here was the ideal résumé for someone to lead Newport's architecture into its golden age. He was an artist astute at both real estate and public relations.

Mason set a crucial trend early in the game. Like others, he recognized Newport's attraction as a summer colony. But he also envisioned it as few had before—as a magnet for the very best minds in the country and a place where they could interact and stimulate one another. He urged some of his artistic and academic friends to consider the Kay-Catherine-Old Beach Road area as the place to build a summer home, and under his influence this special place began to be populated with college professors, authors, artists, and other persons of culture. Among these were Thomas Gold Appleton, Boston essayist and poet; Kate Wormeley, gifted translator and founder of the precursor to the Red Cross; Charlotte Cushman, actress and singer of international fame; John La Farge, painter and stained glass artist; Maud Howe Elliot, writer and founder of the Newport Art Association; Julia Ward Howe, author of "The Battle Hymn of the Republic"; and Professor William Barton Rogers, himself an artist, architect, and writer, and a founder of MIT. Mason

George Champlin Mason House, 1872, Mason & Mason, Sunnyside Place

did much to enhance the artistic life of Newport. His own home, a chalet called Woodbine Cottage on Old Beach Road, incorporated the very best of woodworking skills.

In addition to his other talents, George Mason had a profound interest in history. Thus, he looked to the first builders in Newport with a great deal more respect than was usual for his time. He loved to gather historic information and pass it on through his writing, both in books and in the newspapers that he edited. He was an intellectual and, by virtue of this, sought the company of others who also were thinkers. Together, Mason and his friends and colleagues helped build Newport of the nineteenth century.

Fort Adams Commandant Headquarters

mason's architectural legacy

Mason had returned to his native city in time to see the Greek Revival architects' work completed and to appreciate the magnificent stonework of Alexander MacGregor. He witnessed the first of Richard Morris Hunt's designs.

Mason's first houses were quite ambitious. In 1860, he designed Starboard House on Narragansett Avenue. This large stone edifice speaks of what Mason witnessed around him—MacGregor's Perry Mill, standing solidly on the corner of Levin and Thames Streets; Swanhurst, a house built at Bellevue Avenue by MacGregor for Judge Swan in 1851; Chateau-sur-Mer, built by Seth Bradford in 1853 out of granite from

Chateau-sur-Mer, 1853, Seth Bradford, Bellevue Avenue

Fall River, Massachusetts. Starboard House belonged to Edward Ogden and was one of seven houses Mason built along Narragansett Avenue.

Although this first design was of stone, Mason had a special interest in building with wood, and many of his early, ambitious designs reflect this. Chepstow (Narragansett Avenue) was built of wood with butted joints to resemble stucco. On Gravel Court (also on Narragansett Avenue), Mason employed undisguised clapboards.

Mason felt that wood was best utilized in Swiss chalets, as in Hunt's chalet on Halidon Hill. In 1873–74, Mason and his son, George Jr., built Woodbine Cottage on Sunnyside Place, using the Swiss chalet context but infusing the whole with an incredible lacework of Carpenter Gothic scrollsaw embellishment on the balcony. Mason designed other chalets in the 1870s; the Edward Cunningham House (1 Cottage Street), built in 1871–72, is a good example, and has recently been refurbished.

As the 1870s progressed, the Mason firm built larger wooden houses. Each sported a verandah, allowing the owner to be in touch with the outdoors and nature. The house now called the Eisenhower House at Fort Adams is one of these, as is the Chanler House, now stuccoed and known as the Cliff Walk Manor, overlooking Easton's Beach.

Mason & Mason were asked to replace the Atlantic House with a residence for Seth B. Stitt, and the resulting structure, now used as an Elks Lodge, is a masterpiece of curving verandahs, massed forms, a tower, and exceptionally intricate detail.

Perhaps the high point of Mason's wood design was Heartsease, built for C.N. Beach on the corner of Ayrault and Kay streets. This large, rambling structure is full of architectural surprises—curving arches with dentils, a tower, porches, and other details, while all the time holding a very rational massing of building composition.

One of the Masons' most exotic structures is the old Thayer School (the first Rogers High School), built in 1872–73 to resemble a Venetian palace, complete with tower and variegated brick patterns. Its general aspect resembles the first Museum of Fine Arts, built by John Hubbard Sturgis, in Copley Square, Boston. Sturgis completed 10 Redwood Street in Newport in 1863–64 and had designed several other structures (Greenvale Farm, Frederick Rhinelander House, Edith Wharton's house Land's End at 42 Ledge Road, and John Carey's Garden Cottage at 523 Spring Street) so his work was well-known to Mason.

Jeremiah Stitts House, 1879, Mason & Mason, Pelham Street

Sarah Zabriskie House, 1889, Mason & Mason, Rhode Island Avenue

As time passed, the Mason firm built some eclectic houses, purposely blending two or more styles together, as on Stone Gables (100 Rhode Island Avenue). A stone manor house of decidedly Dutch influence, it was designed in 1889 for Sarah Zabriskie. Luce Hall, the large stone edifice on the Newport naval base, is still perhaps the best-known of Mason's designs, completed shortly before George Mason Sr.'s death in 1894.

W.G. Weld House, 1881, Dudley Newton, Bellevue Avenue

dudley newton: mason's apprentice

Dudley Newton, a six-year apprentice of George Mason, went into business for himself at age twenty-one, in the mid-1860s. Born in Newport in 1845, not much has been written about the private life of this wonderful architect. Newton became famous for the so-called Newton roof, a new way to structure the mansard by allowing a space of about 1 foot to extend below the regular roofline above the gutter. This innovation was practical: water could never back up to freeze under the slates or shingles. This patented design soon sprang up all over town.

As Newton's architectural career broadened, he received commissions first for businesses and later for very extensive houses. His design for the Saint Spyridon church in 1865 garnered attention, and he was soon busy creating a building for the Newport police station (1866–67), and a cast-iron front design for the Newport Gas Company (1874–75.) Cornelius Vanderbilt recognized his talent and hired him to do some work on Oakland, the Vanderbilt's country house.

One of Newton's best-known houses is the Harold Brown House (Bellevue Avenue), built of stone in 1893–94 with landscape architecture by the firm of Frederick Law Olmsted. Newton was also commissioned by James Van Alen to co-design Wakehurst, a house near The Breakers on Ochre Point. Newton and the English stained-glass maker Charles Earner Kempe collaborated (1888–89) on this complex and intricate Elizabethan prodigy house. Some of Newton's most interesting work, however, was produced early in his career.

Dudley Newton's studio (20 Bellevue Avenue) is a little jewel. It looks today much as it did in the late 1800s. The bay window, the diamond-shape panes, the variegated tiles on the roof, plus Newton's patented roof design all serve as advertisement for his taste and judgment. Shaped a bit like a shoebox—long and narrow, with only a small facade to the street—the building extends back almost 100 feet into the block.

An outstanding example of Newton's stick style is the Cram House, often called the Jacob Cram or Sturtevant House (Purgatory Road, Middletown), 1875–76. Overlooking Second Beach near the crest of St. George's Hill, this house was built for Mrs. George Clarence Cram and shows off a multitude of angular shapes. The sharp delineation of corners gives a special energy to the crisp design. A broad porch extends its space. In old photographs, the porch is clad in lattice pierced by framed, circular holes. The color of the house was dark red until the 1950s, when it was painted white.

The George Norman complex of buildings (34 Old Beach Road) is built around a main house designed by Seth Bradford in 1850 for H. Allen Wright. It was purchased by George H. Norman the following year. In the 1870s, Dudley Newton created the addition, which is a bit more elegant than the original simple gable, and a most interesting set of outbuildings. The carriage house harks back to the fantasy of King Arthur. The

Jacob Cram House, circa 1870, Dudley Newton, Purgatory Road, Middletown

Belair Carriage House, circa 1870, Dudley Newton, Old Beach Road

little stone house has a tall dunce-cap tower and a fully crenellated tower on the right—now obscured under a green coat of ivy. Just down the driveway toward the gate is a little English cottage covered in vines and sporting elegant gingerbread.

Henry Swinburne House, 1875, Dudley Newton, 97 Rhode Island Avenue

Dudley Newton's delight in houses with many opposing angles and planes is also evident in the Henry Swinburne House (97 Rhode Island Avenue), which utilizes the Swiss chalet design. Newton's treatment of facades here shows his inventiveness while also demonstrating how dynamic the stick style can be. The Henry Swinburne House is delightfully complex in roof design, ornament, and texture. It makes a compelling statement about the integrity of wood construction as developed with the stick style.

The William Smith House, 1872, Dudley Newton, Pelham Street

The chalet on Rhode Island Avenue is extraordinarily free in its asymmetry. It is quite like Newton's Cram House in its generous porch, which seems to gather in the extra space, incorporating it into the main body of the structure. The rooms are clearly delineated on the exterior walls; yet the entire structure is a well-articulated, organic whole.

Newton seems to have relished complex design, at least for a time. The William Smith House (Pelham Street, beside Channing Church) is a good example of how a house can be broken into many different prism shapes and irregular rooflines and still hangs together. Here, the stick style is again wonderfully crisp, the edges sharp, and the relationship of shapes all-important.

Hawkhurst, 1882, Dudley Newton, Kay Street and Cranston Avenue

hawkhurst

One of the most elaborate commissions given to the Newton firm was Hawkhurst, or Hawxhurst (the spelling that is inscribed on one of the gateposts). This very large house, built in 1882 on the corner of Kay Street and Cranston Avenue for Caroline Seymour, is a fascinating composite of gables, complex angles, balconies, and dormers. Its size and rambling shape epitomize the kind of building created in the opulent era of the 1880s. No expense was spared in its construction.

The time of the mansions had not yet fully arrived, so Hawkhurst spoke in an American vernacular, rather than in

Bethshan, 1883, Dudley Newton, 396 Gibbs Avenue

the pseudo-European language of a later time. Hawkhurst's style is Queen Anne: the gables were huge, the textures rich, and the chimneys and towers elaborate.

A building's history often summarizes a city's changes. Such is the case with Hawkhurst. The house passed from Seymour into the hands of the Gray family, and during the First World War it was used as quarters for nurses from the naval hospital. The stock market crash brought the opulent era to a close, and during the Great Depression, Hawkhurst was divided into four smaller sections, with each section relocated to a separate lot and sold separately.

This view looking down Kay Street shows Hawkhurst buildings one, two, and three, which were separated from the massive Hawkhurst structure in 1930. Numbers one and two are made up of pieces of the original building, plus additions. Number three burned to the ground and a new structure was erected on the same footprint.

The original Hawkhurst footprint is depicted with a

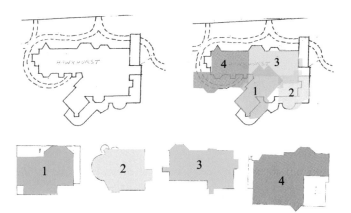

black outline. The colored shapes represent the four sections, as they are believed to have fit together. Note that extra pieces have been added to each of the sections.

The house that today stands at 68 Kay Street must have been the northwest section of the old house. The inside parlor has a coffered paneling that is quite similar to the entry of Bethshan, the Gibbs family house on Gibbs Avenue.

Newton's architecture runs the gamut from the simple townhouse, which seems ubiquitous in the downtown area—to mansions like Hawkhurst on Kay Street, the Benjamin Rhodes House at 45 Everett, The William Smith House at 45 Pelham, and Newton's own house at 52 Division Street—to rambling houses in more suburban settings. One example of the latter is the gracious Bethshan (at 396 Gibbs Avenue), built for Maj. Theodore Kane Gibbs. Commanding a fine view of Easton's Beach, this house is made of stone and brick, with the corners intertwined as the fingers of two hands. The main thrust of the design was the gambrel roof, an element used in the Colonial era.

The William Smith House, the Belair Carriage House, Hawkhurst, Henry Swinburne House, and Bethshan are beautiful examples of an inventive vernacular architecture that seemed to thrive in the fertile Newport soil. Concentrating their work in the northeast section of town, Newton and

George Champlin Mason led the way in developing a grand architecture that is both modest and complex. They were hard-working architects who built practical, durable structures; but they also possessed vision and creativity that added a distinctive flair and style to Newport.

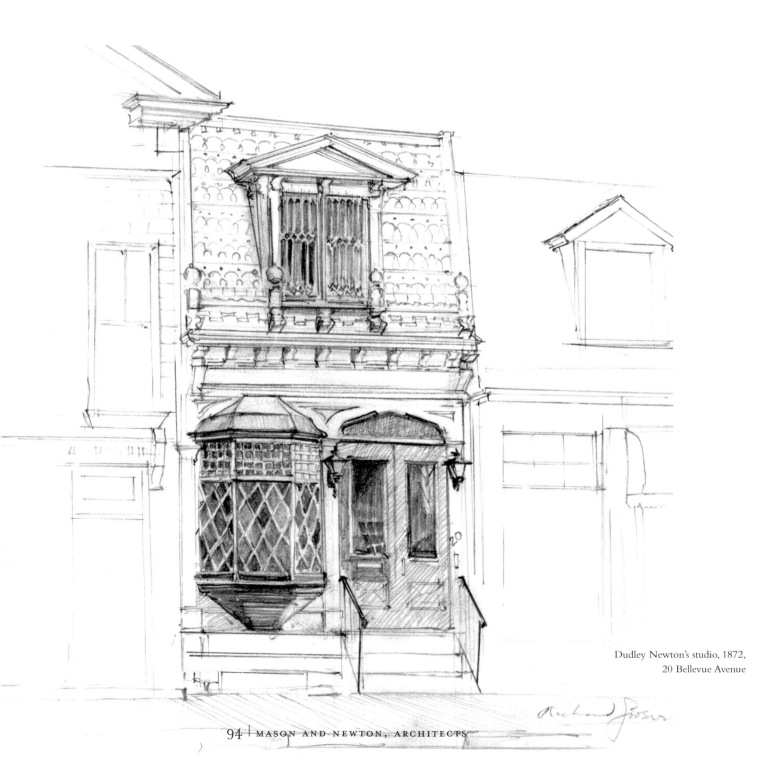

Dudley Newton's studio, 1872,
20 Bellevue Avenue

The William Smith House and Channing Memorial Church, Pelham Street

newport and the search for
an american architecture

Architectural giants Henry Hobson Richardson, Richard Morris Hunt, and the firm of McKim,

Mead, and White found Newport fertile ground in their search for an architecture of substance

that would be used as a pattern for an American style.

William Watts Sherman House, 1874–75, Henry Hobson Richardson, 33 Shepard Avenue

Frank W. Andrews House, 1872–73, Henry Hobson Richardson, Maple Avenue, Middletown

henry hobson richardson

Richardson was one of the most influential architects on the American scene in the latter part of the nineteenth century. Henry Hobson Richardson defined American architecture in his time and in the later years of the nineteenth century. His birthplace in the Deep South, Louisiana, plus his education both in Paris and in Cambridge, Massachusetts, had a great hand in developing his future. He went to college at Harvard, where he made good friends and, as it turns out, many valuable connections. Then he crossed the ocean and enrolled in Paris in the *Académie des Beaux-Arts*. The Civil War arrived while Richardson was there and he found himself in a quandary. He couldn't exactly return to New England and join the forces of the Union, as his entire family was in Louisiana, nor could he join the Confederacy, as all his friends were in the North. He followed advice to stay in Europe until it was over. Richardson's architectural career was truly launched by the winning of (in 1872), and completion of (1877), his first—and perhaps most influential—commission, Trinity Church in Boston. After this, he designed Sever Hall, at Harvard, and five buildings for the Ames family in Easton, Massachusetts. Richardson worked on public buildings, including libraries, and in so doing, set an example of the skillful handling of massive forms that influenced the design of buildings throughout the United States well beyond the short span of his lifetime.

His work was the most creative of the period; he promoted a heavy, rusticated stone style based in both the Romanesque and the Renaissance. His buildings were constructed in great profusion in and around Boston, and in a great many other places around the country. His style, both warm and ponderous, is unmistakable.

Richardson designed only four buildings in Newport—though his influence there is extended through Stanford White, who trained under him. Although he is famous for building with stone, only one of the Newport four was so constructed; nevertheless, they heralded two styles that were important—the Queen Anne and the Richardsonian Romanesque.

The Frank W. Andrews House, originally at Sunset Avenue but no longer extant, was built at almost the same time Richardson was building Trinity Church in Boston. Architectural historian Jeffrey Karl Ochsner draws the connection between the two buildings:

> *The Andrews House was designed at a crucial moment in the development of Richardson's personal vocabulary. The contemporary Trinity Church design has been characterized as a watershed in Richardson's development and the Trinity competition drawings have recently been shown to demonstrate that Richardson was struggling to achieve his own personal synthesis of the principles that he learned in France with the picturesque forms of English work. Perhaps a similar process on a smaller scale explains the Andrews design.* (Journal of the Society of Architectural Historians, *March 1894*)

The Frank W. Andrews House, also called Sunset Lawn, was built in 1872–73 on Sunset Avenue, later Maple Avenue, in Middletown. It was razed in the 1920s. It looks forward to a distinctly stick and Queen Anne style, a stage in Richardson's development. The house featured elements of a "living hall." Ochsner wrote that though this element was derived from English and French sources, it came to full flower in Richardson's world.

> The use of the living hall as the central plan element, around which more specialized spaces were clustered and within which dramatic contrast and focus were established by the massive fireplace and sculptural stairs, was fully achieved as the heart of the Andrews design.

To quote from *Buildings on Paper,* by William H. Jordy and Christopher P. Monkhouse, published by R.I.S.D in 1982,

> *The house, commissioned by Bostonian Frank W. Andrews, was pulled down in the 1920s but is preserved in these drawings, and in some recently discovered photographs. It paralleled in the domestic realm the stylistic direction suggested by Trinity. The design echoed English Queen Anne ideas. The hall-centered plan developed that of the Codman House project, and the clapboarded and shingled exterior continued the swing toward a more coherent external surface which mark the mature Shingle Style. It is the Andrews House Massing that is prophetic however. Its additive plan generated a variety of three-dimensional forms, but as in Trinity, Richardson here began to discipline the irregularities of the picturesque silhouette into a unified pyramidal one.*

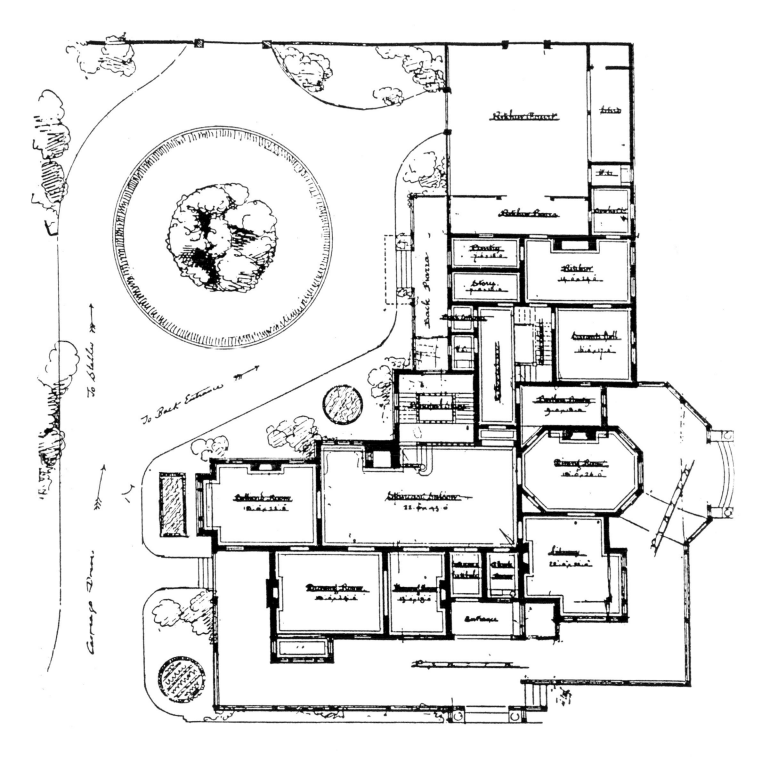

Frank Andrews House plan, 1872, Henry Hobson Richardson

Watts Sherman House, 1875, Henry Hobson Richardson, 33 Shepard Avenue

The living hall was also one of the prime elements in the William Watts Sherman House, which was Richardson's second local design.

The Watts Sherman House (33 Shepard Avenue), built in 1875, is perhaps the best example of the "living hall" in the country. The great hearth in the living hall is lined with Delft tiles. The walls are resplendent with applied gold leaf, and the ceiling is supported by great beams.

The library was added in 1880 by the architect Stanford White, a former colleague of Richardson, who had joined architects Charles Follen McKim and William Rutherford Mead. Elegant with White's inventiveness, the room is punctuated with a highly finished lacquer of green with gold trim.

The Victorian penchant for mystery and novelty is reflected in innumerable small, hidden cubby holes. Panels in a mirror open to disclose small spaces for storage. Above the doors are shell patterns that swing open. This library is a truly delightful room, and in the playfulness of its reed and bamboo patterns, it holds the germ of Art Nouveau designs.

After its years of private ownership, the Watts Sherman House was used as a retirement home for the elderly, run by the Baptist Church, and now is a dormitory for Salve Regina University.

the mason house and
castle hill lighthouse

The last house in which Richardson was involved was commissioned by the Misses Mason and constructed on the corner of Rhode Island Avenue (what was then Bath Road). It had been designed by Seth Bradford for Robert Means Mason. Mason's daughters asked Richardson to renovate it in 1883. The grounds were landscaped by Frederick Law Olmsted. The house burned down around the turn of the century, and a new building by Irving Gill was erected on the site. The Gill building is now St. Michael's School. No plans or photographs exist of the Mason House, and therefore, its size, shape, and influence are matters of conjecture.

A fourth Newport structure designed by Henry Hobson Richardson is Castle Hill Lighthouse, at the entrance to Narragansett Bay. The lighthouse was built some years after Richardson's death. It is quite different from the original plan. This drawing was made for the U.S. Coast Guard and Alexander Agassiz. Richardson designed a short lighthouse to please Agassiz, who felt that anything tall would interrupt his view. The light that guards the entrance to Narragansett Bay still operates and, even though it is set low on the cliff, is still visible at sea. Castle Hill's owner was Alexander Agassiz, son of Louis Agassiz, a legendary professor at Harvard who had infamous disagreements with Charles Darwin.

Castle Hill Lighthouse

Alexander was a biologist and mineralogist who discovered a huge copper lode near Lake Superior.

The key to understanding Richardson's greatness is to observe the number of buildings, both contemporary and later, that bear his mark. His own output was prodigious, and a great many other architects produced plans that should be labeled Richardsonian Romanesque. Today, there are hundreds, if not thousands, of libraries, train stations, and city halls that bear witness to Richardson's vision of massive proportions, rusticated stone work, and pyramidal massing. His was a most distinctive and powerful style.

Linden Gate, The Marquand House, 1873, Richard Morris Hunt,
Rhode Island Avenue

richard morris hunt

Of all architects involved in Newport, perhaps Richard Morris Hunt is best-known. He is important for a number of reasons. His work is a highly visible presence from urban centers like New York to more farflung locales like Asheville, North Carolina. Among his accomplishments are Newport's The Breakers, The Biltmore in North Carolina, and New York's Metropolitan Museum of Art. Hunt was the most celebrated architect of his day and as Jordy and Monkhouse put it in their book *Buildings on Paper,* also champion of his profession. His father was a congressman who died when Hunt was only three. The young boy was brought up under the influence of an artistic mother, who took him to Europe in 1843, after his father's death. He was the first American to attend the *Académie des Beaux-Arts* and then he apprenticed to an architect named Hector Lefuel. It was during this time that he had an opportunity to work on remodeling part of the Louvre. Later, he came back to the United States and established himself in New York in 1855. In 1860, he married Catherine Clinton Howland. He was involved in a great many projects besides being an architect. He founded the American Institute of Architects, and he was instrumental in developing a code for architects that included how they should charge for their services. He was able to give them the legal force needed to establish them as a respected profession. He founded an atelier that included such great men as Henry Van Brunt, George Post, and Frank Furness. "He was a man in tune with his time."

Richard Morris Hunt was well-organized, driven, perfectionistic, and high-minded. When he started practicing in Newport, he had just finished his education at the *Académie des Beaux-Arts* in Paris. This highly disciplined school of architecture indoctrinated its pupils with a strong Classical tendency, a tendency that comes through in Hunt's mature work. His first efforts in Newport were based on a love of the medieval townhouses he had encountered in his European travels. He arrived in Newport at a time when the currents of wealth were beginning to flow into Aquidneck Island, thanks to the profits of the Industrial Revolution. This money was very important in allowing a rather experimental and free practice in the field that otherwise could have been modest and constricted.

John N. A. Griswold House, 1863, Richard Morris Hunt, 76 Bellevue Avenue

A plot of land at the corner of Old Beach Road and Bellevue Avenue became the site of a house Hunt built in 1863 for John N. A. Griswold. It would become the Newport Art Association in 1916 and, in the 1980s, became the Newport Art Museum (76 Bellevue Avenue). Hunt returned from Europe just prior to starting this commission, and the design reflects his love of the medieval European townhouse and his vision that the United States needed a more dignified architecture. There is a dynamic in Hunt's choice of diagonal struts and exposed skeleton. This was the germ of inspiration for Mason and Newton, and the stick style. At the same time, the half-timbered walls are old European forms, representing a dignified pattern, tried and true for centuries.

A look at the Griswold plan (page 107) shows a great open area. From the front door, space is all. The entrance hall affords a view up the full three stories of the building, as the staircase frames the entry and atrium and goes all the way to the roof.

The geometric plan of the space gives strength and unity to the building, but there is variety in the treatment of each room. The Griswold house is not tedious in any way. For example, each floor is a different parquet pattern. The parquet in the hall creates a striped pattern. To the right at the top of the stairs is the library, which is darker and richer than the rest of the rooms. The window shutters are cut with plant forms, and the ceiling is blue with gold stars.

To the right, as you enter the room, originally was an interior window that looked out on the next room—today's Wright Gallery. An interior window was placed above each fireplace, with space on each side for the chimney flues. This made the walls transparent.

What was the Griswold dining room is now the Drury Gallery, cheerfully restored in recent years. It had been painted black over the years, so that the fanciful details disappeared; restoration revealed the image of two of the Griswold's dogs' heads carved in the fireplace.

Richard Morris Hunt's early work in the 1860s and early 1870s was a search for an American architecture that no one had yet devised. European models were fine points of departure. But Hunt's innovative treatment of interiors, and his fanciful, almost storybook exteriors, reflect a permanence which was important. They lent a respectablity to these new houses and placed them squarely on the landscape of nineteenth-century America, where appearances were everything. Such were the houses of the Kay–Catherine–Old Beach Road neighborhood, owned by moderately wealthy intellectuals. The Travers Block, an example of Hunt's early work (1870–72), marches down Bellevue Avenue from Memorial Boulevard to The Casino in fine style.

Richard Hunt's later buildings—especially his mansions of the Gilded Age—were totally different in nature. In the late 1880s and 1890s, he built huge houses for the wealthy. These were the days of ostentation, when there was no federal income tax and money was piled upon money. The wealthy of this era thought of themselves as royalty and needed palaces to prove their worth. They were much more interested in copying the extravagant Baroque styles of Europe than in allowing some architect to experiment with a vital, forward-looking American architecture.

A VISIT TO THE GRISWOLD HOUSE IN 1863

Kate Hunter, a woman of Newport, kept a diary from the middle of the nineteenth century until her death in 1910. On December 31, 1863, at the age of about fifteen, she visited the home of John N.A. Griswold and wrote the following passage. It appears that finishing touches were still being made on the Griswold home— and that Newport itself was as charming as ever.

The last day of the year, tomorrow will be 1864. What a year this has been, as I look back. . . . I asked Papa this morning to meet me at the Redwood Library at 2 o'clock. . . . He and I took a little walk around Kay Street and then back again towards Fowler's—met Fannie O. opposite the park. Fannie had not been to Mr. Griswold's, so we all went over to it. The front stairs have been made since I was there, and there were many other signs of its having progressed. We met Mr. Griswold in the house. We went with him on the roof, where

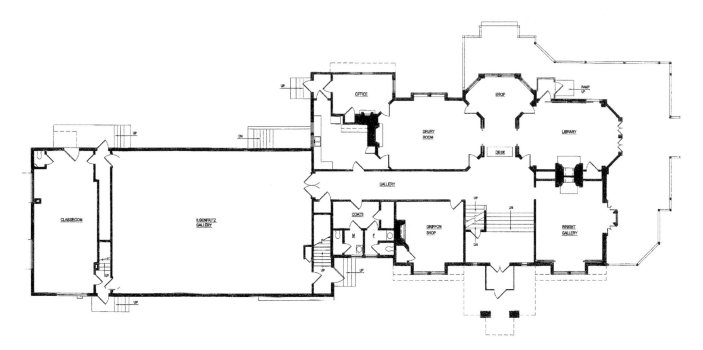

Griswold House plan

is a most magnificent view. On the west is the harbour, the fort, the school ships, and numerous islands, and far over at the Rhode Island shore, there are other islands, and we could even see Prudence, 10 miles up the Bay. The ocean was at the south, with the white sails in the distance, and between it and ourselves were the beautiful villas and country seats of our wealthy citizens and our summer residents. We could see the first, second and third beaches, and the mainland beyond them all. Then on the north east, far into the country. The town was at our feet; opposite, were the Atlantic House [now the Naval Academy] and little Touro Park, with the Old Stone Mill in its center, the Ocean House up the Avenue, also the Fillmore and Bellevue Houses, side by side. The Redwood Library, almost close to us, was hidden by the late Mr. P. Abbot Lawrence's house, which is next to it.

mckim, mead, and white

The Kay-Catherine-Old Beach Road neighborhood is a wonderful repository of history. A number of architects worked in this area. It was the place where they built their first houses and developed their direction. The Griswold House is one of Hunt's first stick style houses. Likewise, some of the most telling examples of the early work of McKim, Mead, and White still stand on Red Cross Avenue.

At the top of the avenue, the Wormeley House, designed almost entirely by Charles Follen McKim, sports an onion top and exotic dome. This is a salute to Miss Wormeley's great interest in travel, as in nowhere else but the Near East would there exist such a shape. To bring this style home to Newport speaks volumes about the thirst for travel and adventure common in those days.

Katherine Wormeley House, 1876-77, Charles Follen McKim,
Old Beach Road and Red Cross Avenue

Frances L. Skinner House, 1882, McKim, Mead, and White,
6 Red Cross Avenue

Samuel Coleman House, 1882–3, McKim, Mead, and White,
6 Red Cross Avenue

The Frances L. Skinner House (6 Red Cross Avenue) is a remarkable amalgam of the small and the monumental, also designed by Charles McKim. The massing of the structure revolves around the squat and solid tower. The roof angles and chimneys provide a lively variety. McKim, Mead, and White built this house at the northern end of the lot to ensure that the owners could take full advantage of the sunny southern landscape. Indeed, most of the properties on the street seem to have been designed with this in mind. The shape, solid proportions, and surface textures of the Skinner House owe a great debt to Henry Hobson Richardson.

Many residences designed by McKim, Mead, and White are concentrated in this neighborhood. Red Cross Avenue itself runs through what was once the Sears estate. Maps made before 1876 show the Sears property with its long drive emanating from a gateway that stood at the jog in Old Beach Road. Later, this drive was paved and lengthened to form Red Cross Avenue. Whitestone, called Oakwood on the maps of the time and built for George Gordon King, is a very large example of Colonial-revival style standing close to the old Sears House, which still exists. With its small pebbled walls, it represents one of McKim, Mead, and White's experiments with textures.

Across the street and a bit farther south at 7 Red Cross Avenue stands the Samuel Coleman House (1882–83) also designed by McKim, Mead, and White. This beautifully proportioned Colonial revival house has a gambrel roof. Again,

Tilton House, 1880–81, McKim, Mead, and White, 13 Sunnyside Place

the lot extends off to the south, and the texture of the shingles and the porches and verandahs add up to a warm and welcoming structure.

Around the corner from Red Cross Avenue, at 13 Sunnyside Place, is a half-timbered house. This is the Tilton House, built by McKim, Mead, and White in the 1880s. What strikes the eye immediately is the overwhelming texture of its wall. There are pieces of broken glass, bottle ends, and rustic wood beams—all juxtaposed—in one facade. The weaving undulation of the wall works well with the shingles. Inside the house, the wood paneling is, surprisingly, redwood—a soft, but handsome, wood hardly ever used for interiors. This architecture, developed near the end of the nineteenth century, represents a subtle, but clear, statement, fulfilling the needs of the client, while using materials imaginatively and effectively. The European influence blends with elements from the American Colonial in these works of McKim, Mead, and White. They were architects of great imagination and sensitivity.

Newport Casino, 1879–81, McKim, Mead, and White, Bellevue Avenue

The Newport Casino (1879–81) exemplifies the shingle style developed to its highest point. Supposedly built on the angry whim of James Gordon Bennett, after he had been reprimanded by his club, the Newport Reading Room, The Casino is a landmark, both socially and architecturally. It holds its place on Bellevue Avenue in the center of the most fashionable part of the city. The entrance from the avenue is a monumental one, rich with tile pavement, staircase, and embellishments. It is a constricted passage, however, so that the sudden break onto the inner court green with its tennis courts and open-air bandstand beyond offers a dramatic experience. The shapes of the inner tower, the verandahs, and the dormers flow with the kind of movement that only the shingle style provides.

The shingle style was a sensuous way of building. The towers are rounded; the dormer windows are like sleepy, half-opened eyes. Facades did not lack for variety, as the thin wood was cut in a great number of shapes. These shapes multiply like

Newport Casino (detail), 1879–81, McKim, Mead, and White, Bellevue Avenue

the scales of fish, covering the gradual curves of the buildings. But this is only half of the story, as, in the case of the Newport Casino, most of what makes up the complex is open air. The role of the Casino architects was to mold negative space and, in a masterly fashion, to make great sense of the solid areas and the voids. It was done beautifully.

We cannot end our discussion of McKim, Mead, and

White without mentioning one of their great masterpieces, The Isaac Bell House. It is one of the most sensitively conceived and executed plans, exhibiting the flowing characteristics of the highly tuned shingle style. This structure, mentioned above in reference to the Queen Anne Style because of its "living hall," is also noteworthy because of the architect's choice of organic elements and rounded shapes. The tower and the adjacent entranceway to the verandah are described with a sweeping curve. The Isaac Bell House, is perhaps the most outstanding example of the shingle style in America.

On Old Beach Road, quite near the shingle style houses designed by McKim, Mead, and White, stands the Commodore Edgar House—as different from its neighbors as could be. The Edgar House is a monument to the Classical revival of 1886 while borrowing from the grand Colonial summer house, with its almost symmetrical facade. The bricks form a wonderful surface texture of long shapes, in imitation of Roman buildings. The large Classical porch, with graceful columns, gives it a highly formal look. This is in contrast to the informal houses nearby on Red Cross Avenue with their flowing, shingled shapes. Here, the architecture takes an exciting turn with a blend of the Classical and American styles. This change to a substantial, monumental house of masonry points ahead toward the mansions of Bellevue Avenue.

Isaac Bell House, 1881, McKim, Mead, and White,
Bellevue Avenue and Perry Street

Commodore Edgar House, 1886, McKim, Mead, and White,
Old Beach Road

the mansions of newport's gilded age

BELLEVUE AVENUE, running north to south through the most beautiful part of the city, was developed during the Gilded Age. Here, the wealth of the mercantile sea captains of the eighteenth century, so well-represented by their houses on Washington Street, was surpassed by the sophisticated, worldly society of the late nineteenth century. The "cottages" of the very rich were built at a time when self-conscious ostentation was the rule. The values of the European courts found fertile soil here, and "The Avenue" became a showplace for the carriages and fine livery of the Victorian era. Many gardens and estates felt the masterful touch of the father of American landscape architecture, Frederick Law Olmsted. The houses, the gardens, and the avenue itself blend into a harmony unique to Newport. Today, it remains a place of majesty, shaded by trees over one hundred years old and overwhelmed by splendid houses and landscapes.

Gates on Bellevue Avenue.

The *Newport Mercury* (May 15, 1852) described the beginnings of this famous American street:

> The whole face of that portion of the Neck lying between Spouting Horn Beach and Easton's Beach has been been divided and subdivided into building lots, roads have been opened, tens of thousands of trees have been planted, and fine, substantial buildings have gone up as if by magic. Great as has been the improvement, the work is progressing rapidly, and we can look forward to no distant day when the whole south of Newport will present the most charming appearance, equaling in beauty the far famed Isle of Wight.

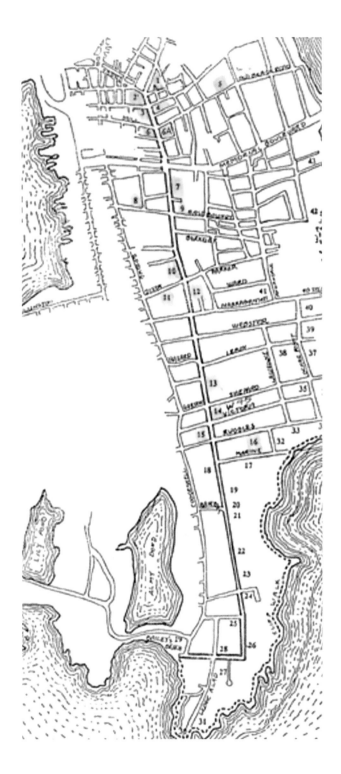

BELLEVUE AVENUE: "The Avenue" encompasses so much of yesterday and today. This list compiled by the Redwood Library on the occasion of the rededication of Bellevue Avenue, in May–June 1992, documents residences that have graced Newport as far back as the seventeenth century.

1. Old Jewish Cemetery, established 1677. Gates, 1842, architect Isaiah Rogers.

2. Hilltop Inn, 1 Bellevue Avenue, now the Viking Hotel.

3. Newport Reading Room, 29 Bellevue Avenue, founded 1853.

4. Redwood Library and Athenaeum, 50 Bellevue Avenue, 1748–50, architect Peter Harrison, expanded 1858 by G. Snell, 1875 by G.C. Mason.

5. Belair (George H. Norman House), 34 Old Beach Road, 1850, architect Seth Bradford; enlarged 1870 by Dudley Newton, stable and lodge built 1875.

6. Touro Park, established 1855, Old Stone Mill ca. 1650s.

6A. Newport Art Museum (John N.A. Griswold House), 76 Bellevue Avenue, 1862–64, architect R.M. Hunt.

7. The Casino, 186–200 Bellevue Avenue, 1879–81, architects McKim, Mead, and White.

8. Edward King House (now the King Senior Center), Spring Street at Bowery Street, 1845–47, architect Richard Upjohn.

9. Ocean House, Bellevue Avenue at Bowery, 1845, architects Russell Warren & Son, burned 1898.

10. The Elms (Edward Berwind House), 350 Bellevue Avenue, 1899–1902, architect Horace Trumbauer.

11. Villa Rosa (Rollins Morse House), 401 Bellevue Avenue, 1900, architect Ogden Codman Jr., razed 1960s.

12. White Lodge (Henry Sigourney House), 412 Bellevue Avenue, 1863–64, architect G.C. Mason.

13. Chateau-sur-Mer (William Shepard Wetmore House), 470 Bellevue Avenue, 1851–53, architect Seth Bradford, enlarged 1869–80 by R.M. Hunt.

14. Vernon Court (Mrs. Richard Gambrill House), 492 Bellevue Avenue, 1899–1901, architect Thomas Hastings.

15. Chetwode (William Storrs Wells House), Bellevue Avenue at Ruggles Avenue, architect H. Trumbauer, burned 1973.

16. Seaview Terrace (Edson Bradley House), Ruggles Avenue at Wetmore Street, 1924–29.

17. By-the-Sea (August Belmont House), Bellevue Avenue at Marine Street, 1860, architect G.C. Mason, razed 1950.

18. Ivy Tower, formerly Snug Harbor (Mrs. Harriet Pond House), 539 Bellevue Avenue, 1887–89.

19. Rosecliff (Tessie Oelrichs House), 54 Bellevue Avenue, 1897–1902, architects McKim, Mead, and White.

20. Seacliffe (Christopher Wolfe House, later owned by T.W. Phinney, Harry Paine Whitney), Bellevue Avenue opposite Bancroft Street, 1852–53, architect Joseph Wells, burned 1942.

21. Beechwood (Daniel Parrish House, later owned by Mrs. William B. Astor), 580 Bellevue Avenue, 1852–53, architects Calvert Vaux & A.J. Downing, enlarged 1890 by R.M. Hunt.

22. Marble House (William K. and Alva Vanderbilt House), 600 Bellevue Avenue, 1888–92, architect R.M. Hunt; Chinese Tea House by Hunt and Hunt, 1912–14.

23. Clarendon Court (Edward Knight House), 620 Bellevue Avenue, 1903–04, architect H. Trumbauer.

24. Miramar (Mrs. George Widener House), 650 Bellevue Avenue, 1912–14, architect H. Trumbauer.

25. Belcourt (Oliver H.P. Belmont House), 657 Bellevue Avenue, 1891–94, architect R.M. Hunt.

26. Rough Point (Fred. W. Vanderbilt House, later owned by Doris Duke), 680 Bellevue Avenue, 1887–91, architects Peabody & Stearns.

27. Rockhurst (Mrs. H.M. Brooks House), 720 Bellevue Avenue, 1890–96, architects Peabody & Stearns, razed 1945.

28. Beach-Mound (Benjamin Thaw House), 729 Bellevue Avenue, 1897–98, architect Henry Ives Cobb.

29. Bailey's Beach, original building by John H. Sturgis, Ocean Avenue, destroyed by hurricane of September 1938.

30. The Breakwater (Gov. Charles W. Lappet House), Ledge Road, 1898–99, architect Robert H. Robertson, razed 1924.

31. Land's End (Samuel G. Ward House, later owned by Edith Wharton), 42 Ledge Road, 1864–65, architect John H. Sturgis.

32. The Cloister (James P. Kernochan House), Wetmore Street at Marine Street, 1885–87, architect J.D. Johnston, razed 1950s.

33. Mid-Cliff (C.O. Jones & L.B. McCagg House), Ruggles Avenue at Lawrence Avenue, 1886, architects Peabody & Stearns.

34. Fairholme (Fairman Rogers House), Ruggles Avenue at Ochre Point, 1874–75, architect Frank Furness.

35. Greystone (Fitch Bosworth House, later owned by John Wysong), Ochre Point at Victoria Avenue, 1882–83, architects G.C. Mason & son, burned 1938.

Bellevue Avenue

36. The Breakers (Cornelius Vanderbilt II House), Ochre Point Avenue, 1892–95, architect R.M. Hunt.

37. Vinland (Catherine L. Wolfe House), Ochre Point Avenue, 1882-83, architects Peabody & Stearns.

38. Wakehurst (James J. Van Alen House), Ochre Point at Leroy Avenue, 1882–88, architects Chas. E. Kempe & Dudley Newton.

39. Ochre Court (Ogden Goelet House), Ochre Point Avenue, 1888–91, architect R.M. Hunt.

40. Ochre Point (Robert Goelet House, erroneously called Southside).

41. Pinard Cottage, Narragansett Street and Ananadale Road, Dudley Newton architect.

42. Hopedene, Cliff Avenue south of Dresser Street, 1899, architects Peabody & Stearns.

43. New Cliff Hotel and Cottages, Cliff Street and Seaview Street, 1889, enlarged 1891–3, burned 1908.

44. Easton's Beach—Memorial Boulevard bathhouses by Peabody & Stearns, 1836–37; Nearby pavilion S.S. Ward, ca. 1879, destroyed by hurricane, rebuilt often.

45. William Watts–Sherman House, Shepard Avenue, 1874–75, architect H.H. Richardson.

newport's mansions

The search for a uniquely American architecture had progressed successfully in the two decades following the Civil War. The heavy Tudor style of the early Richard Morris Hunt designs grew lighter, and the stick style multiplied, in both Richardson's Andrews House and in Dudley Newton's Cram House. Shingles seemed to flow around the buildings of McKim, Mead, and White. The creative, free-flowing designs of the Skinner House, the Isaac Bell House, and the Casino also reflect the genius of American architects.

Newport changed profoundly in the 1890s. The house became an entertainment pavilion. Palaces associated with European aristocracy began to bloom in miniature on relatively small lots along Bellevue Avenue. The architectural inspiration for these unabashedly ostentatious mansions may have come from the 1893 World's Fair in Chicago, known as the Columbian Exposition. The exposition itself has been characterized as the startling stylistic union of classical Greece, imperial Rome, Renaissance Italy, and Bourbon Paris, instigated by the force of America's newfound industrial wealth.

Siegfried Giedion explains the exposition's impact:

> *The 1893 World's Fair elicited a variety of responses. The public and most of the architects were rapturous in their delight. While I was in Chicago, one architect who had worked on it quoted from memory a rather ironical comment of William James: "Everyone says one ought to sell all one owns and mortgage one's soul to go there; it is esteemed such a revelation of beauty. People cast away all sin and baseness, burst into tears, and grow religious, etc., under the influence."*
>
> *Some European observers were more skeptical. An extremely well-informed Belgian constructor, Vierendeel, found both its staff architecture and the construction it enveloped "timid and second-hand."* (Space, Time, and Architecture, *Harvard University Press, 1967*)

Public artists and literary people believed themselves to be witnessing a splendid rebirth of the great traditions of past ages. The immense appeal of this re-created past in the White City may be laid to a quite unnecessary national inferiority complex. This—reinforced by the prestige of the Paris exhibition of 1889—gave French academicians a dominating role at the Chicago fair. A contemporary biographer, John Root, expresses it quite clearly:

> *At that time, few hoped to rival Paris; the artistic capacity and the experience of the French made us distrustful of ourselves. We should have had a great American fair, but in points of grouping and design we must expect inferiority to French taste. And it was to France that the builders of the Fair turned in their search for beauty. Its beauties were taken out of the preserve jars of the* Académie des Beaux-Arts—*where they had been laid up during what was certainly its worst period.*

The influence of the Chicago exposition of 1893 is apparent—although several mansions were begun a few years earlier. Richard Morris Hunt, who was actively engaged in planning the exposition's "Great White City," would have been influenced earlier than other architects working in Newport. Pressure built for mansions that emulated the

Vernon Court, 1898, A.J. Hastings

palaces of Europe. Such designs, promoted by the *Académie des Beaux-Arts* (which Richard Morris Hunt had attended), piqued America's envy of Europe. Richard Morris Hunt built Ochre Court in 1891, Belcourt Castle and Marble House in 1892, and the Breakers in 1895. Horace Trumbauer built the Elms in 1901; and McKim, Mead, and White built Beacon Rock in 1891, and Rosecliff in 1902. The baroque, rococo, and Renaissance styles they embodied were found in Paris and Vienna. Sparing no expense to bring the very best to Newport, Hunt sometimes imported foreign workmen to implement foreign designs and building crafts.

The ostentatious products of America's fin-de-siecle envy and insecurity stand today—in marble, terra-cotta, and limestone—receiving visitors from all nations who come to gaze at our nation's past.

Ochre Court, 1888, Richard Morris Hunt, Ochre Point Avenue

ochre court

Designed by Hunt in 1888 and finished in 1891 for Ogden Goelet, this building is a perfect example of the extravagant use of beaux-arts design. The mansion, built of limestone, incorporates a multitude of details befitting a medieval castle. Scholarly rather than inventive, it demonstrates Hunt's architectural training.

Ochre Court's great hall is carefully calculated to impress. Coming up the stairs from the main door, one is greeted by a three-story atrium. There are three tiers of arches, one above the other, each framing a passageway to the upstairs rooms. The ceiling is supported visually by a rank of caryatids. All this carved and gilded work of half-clad women and cherubs enhances the ceiling that depicts the "Banquet of the Gods." The library, dining room, and ballroom downstairs all lead off from the atrium. Each is resplendent with large fireplaces and decorative ceilings. The large French windows give an unimpeded view of the Atlantic Ocean. The site for the house is small, but the view is seemingly infinite.

belcourt

Belcourt was designed by Hunt for Oliver H.P. Belmont in 1892 with no less a plan than the hunting lodge of Versailles in mind. Mr. Belmont loved his horses, and one major design challenge was to incorporate a stable in the plan for the eclectic mansion. Hunt fashioned a carriage entrance into the house, enabling horses to pass by the foot of the stairs. A courtyard for the stable is capped by a half-timber tower and surrounded by a half-timbered facade

The house itself has a special atmosphere. Upstairs, one encounters carved figures and faces—small grotesques that lend an almost medieval charm. At the top of the stairs, there is a small, elliptical dining room with seating for about ten—one of the most intimate parts of an otherwise very grand home. Large windows expose the dining room completely to the open air. A portrait hall runs along the side of the banquet hall. All the richness of the French Renaissance is reflected in this mansion.

Belcourt, 1892, Richard Morris Hunt, Bellevue Avenue

The Breakers, 1892–95, Richard Morris Hunt, Ochre Point Avenue

the breakers

The largest of the Newport Mansions, The Breakers (1892–95) was modeled after Genoese merchant palaces of the Renaissance. The plan—inspired by Italian Renaissance architect Andrea Palladio, includes a large central court, with rooms leading from it.

Everything about The Breakers is large. The iron entrance gates are 30 feet high, carefully sculptured with scrolls and volutes including the wrought-iron initials *CV* (Cornelius Vanderbilt). There are seventy rooms, of which thirty-three were set aside for the staff. For all its immensity, however, this mansion occupies a relatively small lot. Its size may have been more of an affirmation for Hunt and his prowess as an architect. A monument of this size with its large interior space cannot help but be awe-inspiring.

In 1973, the Preservation Society of Newport County purchased The Breakers from the Vanderbilts.

Marble House, 1892, Richard Morris Hunt, Bellevue Avenue

marble house

Built in 1892 for William Vanderbilt, as a present for his wife Alva, Marble House is as elaborate and costly as any Newport mansion. Its construction was as dramatic as it was expensive. The marble was rare and exotic—Sienna, Breccia, Numidian, and other varieties—most of it imported. The workmen were sequestered until the opening of the house to keep its splendiferousness a secret.

Marble House was designed to be an entertainment pavilion, with a ballroom of carved and gilded wood, great mirrors, and chandeliers. By contrast, the room adjoining presented the severe austerity of Gothic design with a coffered ceiling. The dining room was designed after the Salon of Hercules, in Versailles. The kitchen was remarkably large and equipped for all varieties of French cooking.

Antoinette Downing, co-author of *The Architectural Heritage of Newport Rhode Island*, wrote:

One of the country's great turn-of-the-century classically inspired buildings, Marble House epitomizes the design principles of the Académie des Beaux-Arts. *It emphasizes composition, symmetry, and forms derived from Greece and Rome...From its academic French classical exterior through its classically composed eclectic interiors—ranging from the Louis XIV mode of the Gold Ballroom and the rococo detailing of the library, to the faithful interpretation of the Gothic Room—Marble House reflects a high point in the historicism of the late nineteenth century.*

The Chinese Tea House, 1914, Hunt and Hunt

the chinese tea house

In 1914 the Chinese Tea House was built at the back of the grounds of Marble House, above the Cliff Walk; it was moved in 1977 when it became obvious that the cliffs were deteriorating, threatening to undermine the structure. Richard Morris Hunt's sons were in charge of creating this building. They did extensive research in China and settled on a plan incorporating elements of southern Chinese temple design. About 1992, the structure was inspected and reinforced.

rosecliff

Rosecliff was named for a house that had occupied the site from the 1850s to the 1880s. The owner of the previous house, George Bancroft, was a great fancier of flowers, and the house took its name from his famous rose gardens.

After Bancroft died, his house was sold to Hermann and Tessie Oelrichs, and they commissioned McKim, Mead, and White to replace it with a large, white mansion patterned after the Grand Trianon at Versailles, built for Louis XIV by his architect, Mansart, in 1687–91.

The original estate, Grand Trianon, was a single story. McKim, Mead, and White (perhaps following the lead of Gabriel's Petite Trianon built at Versailles for Madame de Pompadour) incorporated a second floor similar to the French design. Rosecliff, erected in 1899 and 1900, was one of the firm's most-renowned works. It was surfaced with a white terra-cotta, rather than stone. Stanford White had collected a great deal of tile on his trips to Europe, and his use of it here reflected his genius for color and texture.

White was careful to follow the general plan of the Petit Trianon with an "H" floor plan. The top of the "H" included wings that sheltered spaces to the East. White included courts into which the main ballroom opened through beautifully designed arched windows. With the ocean view and the

Rosecliff, 1899 1900, McKim, Mead, and White, Bellevue Avenue

fountain on that side, Rosecliff was complete. The designs were distinctly eighteenth-century French, but perhaps yielding to the American building technology at the end of the nineteenth century, incorporated steel as the structural material for the house.

Tessie Oelrichs was a leader of Newport high society, along with the Vanderbilts, and, as such, it was important for her that her house be well-suited for entertaining. It was at Rosecliff that the Oelrichs held the legendary "White Ball," a party featuring a fleet of hastily constructed dummy white ships moored offshore for effect.

PEABODY & STEARNS

Robert Swaine Peabody, 1845–1917

John Goddard Stearns, 1843–1917

This firm designed buildings across the country, through the South and also New England. They produced more than 1,500 building designs, many of which were quite notable. They designed the Customs House Tower in Boston, 1909–1915, The Brunswick hotel 1874–75, and the Mutual Life Insurance Company of New York Building, 1874–75. They also designed the Machinery Hall building and the Massachusetts State Building at the Columbian Exposition of 1893. In Newport, the following were designed by Peabody & Stearns: Pierre Lorillard's Breakers 1877–79, Catherine Lorillard Wolfe's Vinland 1882–84, William Gammell's Ocean Lawn 1888–89, Frederick Vanderbilt's Rough Point 1887–88, Gawn F. Hutton's Shamrock Cliff 1894–96, and the Fanny Foster House Ridgemere 1897–98, just to name a few. This architectural company was not in the least flamboyant, but their buildings were very substantial and they were important contributors to the Newport scene.

RIDGEMERE 1897–98, By Peabody & Stearns

This house was built for a maiden lady, Fanny Foster. The site was first occupied by a stick style mansard-roofed wooden house built by her father. After her father died, Miss Foster had the house moved to Perry Street and this house replaced it in 1897. This house, built of brick, dominates the landscape at LeRoy Avenue just east of Bellevue Avenue. The design of twin turrets gives the silhouette of this house a strength that perhaps borrows from fortress complexes in Europe. Inside, after entering the house at the front door, you enter into a "living hall" of generous proportions. This hall gives access to beautiful round rooms, a library to your right, and a living room to your left, which are, in fact, the inside of the turrets we discovered on seeing the house from the outside. There is a stairway at the end of the hall with spindels of delicately carved wood, reminiscent of the Colonial manner. As the stairway climbs to the second floor, the balustrade makes graceful "S" curves. The rooms upstairs over the round rooms are bedrooms that are made all the more interesting by their unusual shape. The variation of spaces makes this house most unusual and interesting.

Ridgemere, 1897–98, Peabody & Stearns, Leroy Avenue

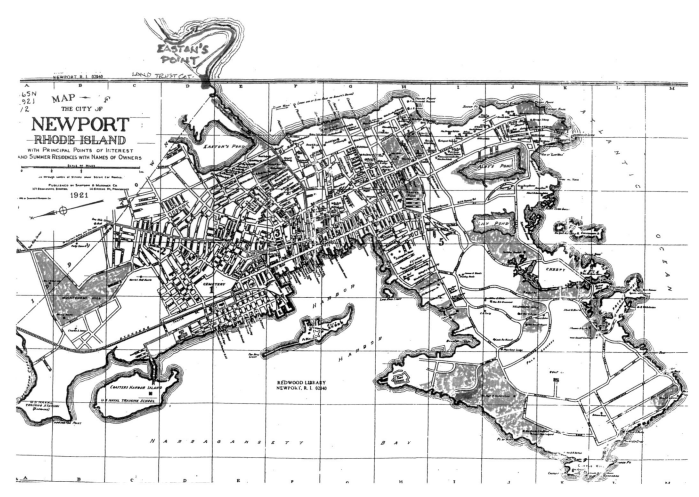

Landscapes (in green) planned by Frederick Law Olmsted or his firm, courtesy of Cindy Brockwayt

frederick law olmsted

Although most of the great houses of Bellevue Avenue were placed on relatively small lots, a great deal of attention and care was given to landscape design and upkeep. Many of the large estates were designed by Frederick Law Olmsted, the genius behind Central Park in New York City and the Emerald Necklace in Boston. Olmsted's view of nature made him one of the first environmentalists. He always worked with nature rather than trying to force it to his will. He felt that his most successful projects hid the fact that mankind had anything to do with the final results. The finished landscape, he thought, should look totally natural. He also felt that landscapes and parks should be beneficial to man. To "recreate" would mean to remove the stress from man's life. Green places within the industrial world would enable mankind to live a good life, and recreation, the all-important balance, took on real meaning.

At the turn of the century, he produced a plan for the entire city of Newport to help adapt the town to modern times, while keeping it environmentally beautiful. The overall design would be of great importance in shaping the twentieth-century city.

The city of Newport asked for a master plan, and the Olmsted firm did its best to supply it. The partners gathered information on everything from traffic statistics to the Newport's population growth. Middletown's designs for Easton's Point and a massive plan for Easton's Beach were both taken into account, though neither was ever realized. The beach plan included an analysis of the South Pond portion of the public reservoir. The Olmsted architects wanted to turn this rather shallow and unused portion of the water supply into islands and lagoons similar to the fens in Boston's Back Bay, which became links in the Emerald Necklace. A circulating highway was envisioned in the place now occupied by the modern America's Cup Highway built in the late 1960s. Other Olmsted ideas included beautifying Broadway and extending Washington Street toward Coddington Cove.

Many improvements never came to pass; sometimes the City Council had other plans, time ran out, or conflicting goals could not be reconciled. However, there were a great many projects that did get completed: the gardens at Harold Brown's estate, the gardens of Chateau-sur-Mer, the entire Easton's Point area; and the long strip of gardens and lawn running along the bay, extending from the John Brown Estate (now the New York Yacht Club) to Pencraig, Bonniecrest, and Beech Bound (the old Ripley estate).

The Transcendentalists of New England had found God in nature. Olmsted seemed to travel a similar path, except that his emphasis was therapeutic, rather than wholly religious. To illustrate the Olmsted influence in Newport, the map shows his projects in green. Frederick Law Olmsted and his firm had a distinct and lasting impact on Newport, and the city gained a great deal by their influence.

Olmsted properties in Newport

Properties designed or influenced by Frederick Law
Olmsted and/or his firm.

OF=Olmsted firm, OB=Olmsted Bros.,

JCO=J.C. Olmsted, FLO=Frederick L. Olmsted

1. Hammersmith Farm OF 1909-46, building 1909

2. Redwood Library (plans never executed)

3. Eisenhower Park OF 1895–1926, Shurtleff 1900

4. Fort Adams OB 1941

5. Chateau-sur-Mer OF 1915–16

6. J.N.A. Griswold House OB 1921

7. Miss Ellen Mason, St. Michael's School

    FLO 1882, 1902–10

8. Anson Stokes estate (Miantonomi)

    FLO 1882–84, OB 1915–21

9. Theodore Davis (Reef Point)

    FLO 1882–1890, building 1882

10. Stoneacre (Bellevue) FLO 1883–1884

11. Easton's Beach/Easton's Point/Bath Road FLO

    1883–1887

12. King, Glover, Bradley (subdivision Ocean to Harrison)

    FLO & JCO 1883, lots between Cherry Neck and

    Brenton Road OB 1915

13. T. Suffern Tailor, Ruggles Ave. FLO 1885

14. Glover residence (Bruce Howe) Berry Hill 1886–87

15. Misses Jones, Ruggles Ave. (Midcliff)

    FLO & JCO 1886–87

16. Newport Hospital Grounds, Carroll Ave. between west

    shore of Almy's Pond and east shore of Cherry Neck,

    including both sides of Ocean Avenue, Carroll Avenue,

    and Lily Pond FLO & JCO 1886–1900

17. Henry Clews Estate FLO, never executed 1886–88

18. Rough Point, Bellevue Avenue FLO 1887–89

19. Ocean Lawn, Narragansett Avenue FLO & JCO 1888

20. Harbor Court, Halidon Avenue OB 1913–15

21. Indian Spring (J.R. Busk residence)

    FLO & JCO 1890–92

22. Ochre Court FLO & JCO 1891

23. Bleak House, Ocean Avenue,

    Ross Winan Estate FLO, JCO 1892–94,

    OB 1909–1906.

24. The Waves FLO & JCO 1892-97

    Lippitt estate, Pope estate OF 1930–31

25. Beech Bound, Burden estate/Ripley

    JCO/Eliot 1893–95

26. Newport Parks, Mall, Morton Park,

    Lemington Beach FLO/JCO/Eliot 1894–95

27. Harold Brown Villa, Bellevue at Hazard

    FLO/JCO/Eliot 1894

28. Wildacre, Albert Olmsted's residence OF 1899–1902

29. King Senior Center (George Gordon King residence)

    OB 1905–6 ,1845–47

30. Bonniecrest, residence of Stuart Duncan, Harrison

    OB 1911

31. Arthur Curtis James estate OB, Old Belvoir Estate,

    FLO/JCO developed the subdivision plan 1889,

    OB did the Blue Garden 1912

32. Proposed improvements for Newport. See above earlier improvements. In 1893, Newport established a Public Parks Commission. Newport Improvement Society contracted FLO Jr. to make a study in regard to public improvements: new railroad station, extension of Washington Street northwards, a circuit drive around the northern part of the city joining Kay Street,widening of Bath Road, creating a park around Almy's Pond, a new street between the waterfront and Thames for relieving the congestion of the latter.

33. Plantings around railroad station grounds OB 1914

34. Vos residence, Zee Rust OB 1915

35. A subdivision directed by A.C. James and J.K. Sullivan. Armsea Hall on Ridge Road, bought by Charles Hoffman, original subdivision FLO & JCO 1888

36. Aspen Hall, Bellevue and Ledge Road

    for John Aspergren OB 1922

37. Eagle's Nest (Frazer Jelke residence) Ocean Avenue

    near Hazard OB 1922.

the twilight of newport's golden age

Architecture is a fascinating visual record of the way people thought in another time. Buildings and their positions in the landscape, both in time and place, send us coded messages about the beliefs, culture, and economics of the era in which they arose. Newport is fortunate that it has attracted such a variety of architecture and that so much of it is intact today.

Bonniecrest, 1912–18, John Russell Pope, Harrison Avenue

The city's fortunes drifted away in the chaos of the two World Wars, which imposed a military sameness to this town with the quartering herein of most of the Atlantic fleet. After World War I, the Navy was served by Newport in much the same way as were scores of other military installations throughout the country. The downtown area witnessed the proliferation of bars and cheap stores catering to the servicemen. In the twenties, the advent of Prohibition augmented the growth of a legendary rum-running trade all through the small inlets and coves that make up the coastline of Aquidneck Island. Narragansett Bay became one of the battlefields of this action. Later, the growth of the Naval War College made a really positive addition to the town. No industry found its way here, except under government control, through the manufacture of torpedoes on Goat Island. During the sixties, the advent of music entertainment appeared in the form of the world famous jazz festivals, followed shortly by the folk festivals, and the more conservative music festival. At the same time, thanks to a political decision by then-President Nixon, the support system for the Navy was moved south, from Boston to Norfolk. This resulted in the departure of the fleet from Narragansett Bay. The town found that its future lay in its rich past . . . in tourism. The world had changed since Newport's Golden Age. Although the changes were interesting, they are there as a subject for another book.

bonniecrest

Bonniecrest on Harrison Avenue, built in 1912–18 by John Russell Pope, is an unexcelled example of Tudor architecture. Its twisted chimney pots and medieval half-timbered shapes rise over Brenton's Cove in Newport's inner harbor. It is a rugged and beautiful statement, fitting a historical style to a natural site. Unfortuately, developers have filled the sloping lawn behind the house with bulky, awkward condominiums that mock the original building's shape. But the house itself remains unchanged outside.

Bonniecrest, 1912–18, John Russell Pope, Harrison Avenue (detail)

The Waves, 1929, John Russell Pope, Ledge Road

the waves

Pope's own home, built by the architect in 1929, replaced a brick-crenellated castle built by Governor Lippett. The old structure was demolished when the governor died, and after Pope bought the site, the old foundation was used for the new house. The building that now overlooks the ocean is in the style of a Norman house. The stonework and the roof, in particular, show a rugged unevenness that endows the structure with tremendous character. The style of a Normandy house is basically a rough stone building with small windows and a slate roof—laid on uneven rafters—that seems to undulate in the sunlight. It's a heavy architecture built to withstand the strong winds of the coast. The chimneys, of which there are unusually many, are also roughly shaped of brick. Some of these houses are made of stucco, half-timbered sometimes, but always full of character.

St. Michael's School, 1902, Irving Gill, Rhode Island Avenue

irving gill

Known best for his work on the West Coast, architect Irving Gill built several houses in Newport. Wildacre on Ocean Drive and the house built originally for the Misses Mason, now St. Michael's School, are distinctly different—the former, a rustic, randomly planned structure, and the latter, an inspired Spanish Colonial.

Wildacre was built for Frederick Law Olmsted's brother, Albert. As heavily rusticated as a stone wall, it is perched on a rocky outcropping bordering a little cove by Price's Neck. The chimney's sharp edges of stone jutt out, while gabled dormers

Wildacre, Irving Gill, Ocean Avenue

are composed in a great variety of angular shapes. It expresses a wildness and natural randomness that is unique and refreshing.

In contrast to Wildacre, St. Michael's School is a Spanish Colonial house placed in a landscape designed by Olmsted. Its tile roof and heavy stucco arches speak of a different time and place—it resembles the type of adobe houses found in the Southwest.

ralph adams cram

Ralph Adams Cram was perhaps the most distinguished and well-known revival architect in this country, so perhaps it is fitting to end with his work. Cram and his partners, Frank William Ferguson and Bertram Grosvenor Goodhue, built Emmanuel Church on Spring Street for the Brown family. This was only the beginning of an association with the Browns. The firm also designed the great French chateau that overlooks the Ida Lewis Yacht Club on Wellington Avenue. It was built originally for John Brown when he was an infant, as the will that governed the funds used to build the house stipulated that the money be used for his benefit. As a result, much of the second floor of the house was devoted to a nursery. The house is now owned by the the New York Yacht Club.

St. George's School Chapel, finished in 1928 in Middletown, is considered Cram's best work. Built on a high piece of land, this magnificent chapel offers a superb view of the beaches and ocean.

The building was commissioned by John Nicholas Brown, a scholar of medieval art and music. The church was designed by Cram to reflect the English Gothic style. A great deal of effort was used to make the symbols and icons in the decorative embellishments meaningful to the times and the young students at the school.

The chapel clearly reflects the amount of care and scholarly effort of both client and architects. John Brown was

Emmanuel Church, 1902–04, Cram, Ferguson, and Goodhue, Spring Street

St. George's School tower, 1928, Ralph Adams Cram,
Purgatory Road, Middletown

twenty-one when he inherited his fortune; as a former student of St. George's, he understood what an important thing he could do for the school and for posterity by building the chapel. He chose one of his classmates, Joseph Coletti, to be the main sculptor for the building. Still a young man, Coletti had just won the Prix de Rome. This enabled him to go to Europe to do extensive research on cathedrals and to choose rare stones for the floor of the St. George's edifice. The floor is resplendent with mosaic work that includes national emblems, state seals of the thirteen original colonies, and signs of the zodiac. The scrollwork pattern at the altar is woven with a wonderful articulation that seems to deny that it is made with stone.

The tower stands 130 feet high on a hill that is another 100 feet above sea level. The vaults of the nave rise to 50 feet above the heads of the congregation. The material used in the building is Indiana limestone. The chapel's construction faithfully follows the plans for typical English Gothic edifices. The crypt is massive and built in heavy Romanesque style—filled with the intersecting arches of the groin vaults, which find purchase in a massive, but short, column in the center. Coletti's carvings on this piece represent the four great rivers of the ancient world—the Gihon, the Tigris, the Euphrates, and the Pison. This recalls Genesis 2:10–14, which tells of a river "that came out of Eden to water the garden and from thence it was parted and became four heads." The title of each waterway is carved

St. George's School, 1928, Ralph Adams Cram, Purgatory Road, Middletown

in the language of its country. The symbolism is carried out on the column: The Gihon is the north side, representing Matthew preaching to the Hebrews; the Tigris is to the west, representing Mark's mission to the Romans; the Euphrates to the South recalls Luke among the Greeks; and to the East is the Pison—John, the herald of all.

The rest of the chapel is light in comparison to the crypt. The enfaced columns in the nave seem to stretch up to the vaults overhead. Light filters in through the stained glass of the side windows. Pier buttresses brace the walls from the outside in true Gothic fashion, though the larger cathedrals of England and France used flying buttresses instead. Only masonry is used, without steel reinforcements, except in the top, over the vaults.

The chapel is full of interesting allusions to contemporary life. At the north entrance to the building, a statue of St. George looks down on two small effigies—a football player

St. George's School Chapter Tower, 1928, Ralph Adams Cram, Purgatory Road, Middletown, as seen from Second Beach

and a baseball player. The history of shipping is carved on the exterior of the cloister in the chapel close on the other side of the church. Ships include a Phoenician galley, a Viking ship, the Spanish ships of Columbus, clipper ships, the first steamship designed by Robert Fulton (the *Clermont*), and a 1928 battleship with an airplane sculpted above it, perhaps in honor of Lindbergh's flight of the year before.

The chapel at St. George's is not the end of the story in Newport, but it ends this book because it marks the end of the nineteenth-century spirit, as it existed here. The chapel was the result of a Gothic revival, and as such is more typical of the nineteenth century than of the twentieth.

This book is an overview of a small city that played a large role in the early years of this great country only to lose its preeminence during the American Revolution. It never recovered its earlier commercial importance, but it came to be especially noted as a magnet for almost all the important architects of this nation, as they served the men made wealthy by the Industrial Revolution. So, in a sense Newport is a wonderful archeological dig, with its many layers of thinking still intact and in place, crystallized in the architecture that still stands here.

selected architects of newport

Aldrich & Sleeper
- 1922-24, Eagle's Nest (Frazier Jelke House), 222 Ocean Avenue

Anderson & Hamilton
- 1879-80, Bluebird Cottage (Mrs. E.G. Hartshorn House), Halidon Hill above Wellington Avenue

Angell & Swift
- 1917, Gooseneck (Jerome C. Borden House; now called Hudson Bay House), 280 Ocean Avenue

Ballantyne and Olson
- 1937, Near Sea, 200 Ocean Avenue

Asher Benjamin (1773-1845)
- 1806, Saint Paul's United Methodist Church, 12 Marlborough Street
- 1817, Rhode Island Union Bank, Thames Street north of Pelham (razed 1952)

E. Boyden & Son
- 1880-81, Channing Memorial Church, 135 Pelham Street

Seth C. Bradford
- 1847-48. Rockry Hall (Albert Sumner House), 425 Bellevue Avenue at Narragansett
- 1850, Belair (H. Allen Wright House; later George Henry Norman House), 34 Old Beach Road
- 1851-53, Chateau-sur-Mer (William Shepard Wetmore House) (enlarged by Richard Morris Hunt, 1869-1880), 470 Bellevue Avenue
- 1852, Robert Means Mason House (burned 1899), formerly at 180 Rhode Island Avenue
- 1852-53, Fairlawn (Mrs. Andrew Ritchie House; later the Levi Parsons Morton House) (enlarged and/or renovated by Richard Morris Hunt, Peabody & Stearns, McKim, Mead & White, and others), Bellevue Avenue at Ruggles
- 1855-56, Old Castle (Alexander Porter House; also called Porter Villa), 25 Greenough Place

C.H. Burdick
- 1881-83, Arthur D. Emmons Stable, Eustis Avenue at Catherine Street

Cabot & Chandler
- 1871-72, Morningside (William Barton Rogers House), 428 Gibbs Avenue

Henry Ives Cobb (1859-1931)
- 1879-98, Beach-Mound (Benjamin Thaw House), 729 Bellevue Avenue

Ogden Codman Jr. (1868-1951)
- The Nunnery, Ocean Avenue at Hazard Road
- 1900-02, Villa Rosa (E. Rollins Morse House), 401 Bellevue Avenue at Dixon Street (razed)
- 1900-03, Faxon Lodge (Frank K. Sturgis House), Cliff Avenue
- 1910, Martha Codman House (Bellevue House or Berkeley Villa), 304 Bellevue Avenue

Interiors only:
- 1893, Edith Wharton House (John Hubbard Sturgis, architect)
- 1893, Harold Brown Villa (Dudley Newton, architect)
- 1895, The Breakers, 2nd & 3rd floors (Richard M. Hunt, architect)
- 1897, Chateau-sur-Mer (Richard M. Hunt, architect)
- 1900, Quatrel (Thomas Alexander Tefft, architect)

Ralph Adams Cram (1863-1942)
- 1902-04, Emmanuel Church, Spring Street at Dearborn (Cram, Ferguson & Goodhue)
- 1903-05, Harbour Court (Mrs. John Nicholas Brown House; New York Yacht Club), 5 Halidon Avenue (Cram, Ferguson & Goodhue)
- 1923-28, Saint George's School Chapel, 372 Purgatory Road, Middletown (Cram & Ferguson)

Daniel W. Curry
- 1889, Dellmain (Mary A.C. Holmes House), 425 Bellevue Avenue at Narragansett (joined to Rockry Hall by Seth C. Bradford, architect)

Alexander Jackson Davis (1803-1892)
- 1848-49, Malbone (Jonathan Prescott Hall House; later Henry Bedlow), Tonomy Hill, Middletown

William Adams Delano (1874-1960)
- 1914, Normandie (Mrs. Lucy Wortham James House), 228 Ocean Avenue
- 1919, Cushing Memorial Gallery, Newport Art Museum, 76 Bellevue Avenue

George M. Dexter

- 1844, Red Cross Cottage (David Sears House) (altered), 8 Oakwood Terrace

Frederic Diaper

- circa 1850, Ralph Izard House, 10 Pell Street
- 1860-61, John R. Ford House, Bowery Street

William Ralph Emerson (1833-1917)

- 1869-70, Milton H. Sanford House (Sanford-Covell House; Villa Marina), 72 Washington Street
- 1882-83, Elm Tree Cottage (Mary Channing Eustis House), 336 Gibbs Avenue
- 1882-83, Mary L. Bruen House (Knight Cottage), 453 Bellevue Avenue
- 1887-89, Land Trust Cottages, Tuckerman Avenue, Middletown (with James Fludder)
- 1890-91, Wyndam (Rosa Anne Grosvenor House), 40 Beacon Hill Road
- 1890-91, Roslyn (William Grosvenor House), 26 Beacon Hill Road

Wilson Eyre Jr. (1858-1944)

- 1884-85, Saint Columba—Berkeley Memorial, 55 Vaucluse Avenue, Middletown

James C. Fludder (1847-1901)

- 1871, Cottages, Torpedo Station (razed)
- circa 1872, Fludder Block Offices and Studio, 22-30 Bellevue Avenue
- circa 1875, John Noble Alsop Griswold Cottage, 29 Champlin Street
- 1876-77, Cave Cliff (George H. Pendleton House), foot of LeRoy Avenue
- 1877, Fire Station #2, 16 Young Street
- 1885, First Baptist Church Parsonage, 30 Spring Street
- 1886-87, Lenthal School, Spring Street near Dearborn
- 1887-88, St. John's Mason Lodge, School and Church Streets
- 1893, Townsend Industrial School, Broadway
- 1901, Carey School, 27 Narragansett Avenue

Frank Furness (1839-1912) (Furness & Evans)

- 1874-75, Fairholme (Fairman Rogers House), Ruggles Avenue
- 1874-75, Fairholme Carriage House (Fairman Rogers Dependency), Ruggles Avenue

Irving Gill (1870-1936)

- Eastover, 144 Wapping Road, Portsmouth
- 1899-1901, Misses Mason House (Saint Michael's School), 180 Rhode Island Avenue
- 1901, Wildacre (Albert Olmsted House), 310 Ocean Avenue
- 1926, The Playhouse (Wildacre Coach House and Boat House), 294 Ocean Avenue

Howard Greenley

- 1924-29, Sea View Terrace (Edson Bradley House; Carey Mansion; Burnham-by-the-Sea), Ruggles and Wetmore Avenues

Harding & Dinkelly

- 1887-88, William H. Osgood House (Preservation Society of Newport County Headquarters), 424 Bellevue Avenue

Peter Harrison (1716-1775)

- 1743, Abraham Redwood Country Estate, West Main Road, Portsmouth (razed)
- 1747, Peter Harrison Farm, Harrison Avenue (extensively altered)
- 1748-49, Redwood Library, 50 Bellevue Avenue
- 1759-63, Touro Synagogue, 184 Touro Street
- 1760-72, Brick Market, Washington Square
- 1766, Abraham Redwood Garden Pavilion, West Main Road, Portsmouth (relocated to grounds of Redwood Library)

Houses probably renovated by Peter Harrison

- 1747-60, Captain John Mawdsley House, Spring and Franklin Streets
- 1748-54, Hunter House (Nichols-Wanton-Hunter House), 54 Washington Street
- circa 1750, Charles Dudley House (Customs Collector Charles Dudley House), West Main Road, Middletown (razed)
- circa 1756, John Banister Country House, One Mile Corner, Middletown (razed)
- 1759-60, William Vernon House, Clarke and Mary Streets
- circa 1760, Francis Malbone House, 392 Thames Street
- circa 1760, Peter Buliod House (later Moses Seixas House and Commodore Oliver Hazard Perry House), 29 Touro Street

Thomas Hastings (1860-1929) (Carrere and Hastings)

- 1898-1901, Vernon Court (Mrs. Richard Gambrill House), 492 Bellevue Avenue at Victoria Avenue

John M. Hodgson

- 1887-88, Lindenhurst (John M. Hodgson House), 434 Bellevue Avenue

Colonel Francis V.L. Hoppin (1867-194)

- 1907, Sherwood (The White House) (Theodore Havemeyer House), 553 Bellevue Avenue (incorporated as the Mrs. Loring Andrews House by George Champlin Mason, 1871-72, later renovated as Friedham by George Champlin Mason & Son)

George Locke Howe (1886-1955)

- 1927-30, Hopelands (T.I. Hare Powel House), Indian Avenue, Middletown

Wallis Eastburn Howe (1868-1960)

Buildings at Saint George's School, Purgatory Road, Middletown

- 1902, Old School Building
- 1911, Auchincloss Gymnasium
- 1920s, Arden Hall, Diman Hall
- 1933, Infirmary

Richard Morris Hunt (1827-1895)

- circa 1860 renovation, William Beach Lawrence House, Ochre Point Avenue (original house by Russell Warren, 1835) (razed 1882)
- 1860-61, Arthur Bronson House, Ocean Avenue at Castle Hill (Ridge Road) (razed 1894)
- 1862-64, John Noble Alsop Griswold House (Newport Art Museum), 76 Bellevue Avenue at Old Beach Road
- 1867-70 renovation, Westcliff (Richard Baker Jr. House), Ledge Road (original house for Charles Mixter House, 1853-54) (razed 1923)
- 1869-70, The Lodge (Mrs. William F. Coles House), Bellevue Avenue at Dixon Street (razed)
- 1869-72, Thomas Hitchcock House (William Travers House), Narragansett Avenue (renovation of an earlier 1860-61 house) (razed 1901)
- 1869-80 renovation, Chateau-sur-Mer (original house by Seth C. Bradford, 1851-53)
- 1870-71, Thomas Gold Appleton House, 45 Catherine Street (burned)
- 1870-71, Hypotenuse House (Richard Morris Hunt House; later Colonel George C. Waring House), 33 Catherine Street at Greenough Place
- 1870-72, Hilltop (Rose and Theodore Phinney House), 95 Ruggles Avenue at Carroll
- 1870-72, William Travers Block, 162-184 Bellevue Avenue
- 1871, Anna M. Gibert House, 651 Bellevue Avenue
- 1871-72, Charlotte Cushman House (Villa Cushman or The Corners), 49 Catherine Street (burned)

- 1871-72, Dr. Charles F. Heywood House, Honyman Hill (Green End Avenue), Middletown (razed)
- 1871-73, Linden Gate (Henry Gurdon Marquand House; Bric-a-Brac Hall), Old Beach Road at Rhode Island (burned 1973)
- 1881-83, Netherwild (Professor Charles W. Shields House), Ruggles Avenue near Lawrence Avenue (extensively altered and stuccoed over)
- 1885, Marquand Family Mausoleum (Island Cemetery), 30 Warner Street
- 1888-91, Ochre Court (Ogden Goelet House), 100 Ochre Point Avenue
- 1888-92, Marble House (William Kissam Vanderbilt House), 600 Bellevue Avenue
- 1889, Ochre Court Carriage House, Lawrence Avenue at LeRoy
- 1889-93, Indian Spring (John R. Busk House; also called Wrentham House), 335 Ocean Avenue
- 1890-91, August Belmont Tomb (Island Cemetery), 30 Warner Street (with Karl Bitter, sculptor)
- 1891-94, Belcourt (Oliver Hazard Perry Belmont House), 657 Bellevue Avenue at Lakeview Avenue
- 1893-95, The Breakers (Cornelius Vanderbilt II House), Ochre Point Avenue

Hunt & Hunt

- 1912-14, Marble House Tea House, 600 Bellevue Avenue on the Cliff Walk

John Dixon Johnston (1849-1928)

- 1881-82, Sea View Villa (General Zachariah C. Deas House), 333 Tuckerman Avenue, Middletown
- 1881-82, Madame M.C. Acosta House, Ochre Point Avenue at Shepard Avenue
- 1882-83, Judge Henry Bookstaver House (also called Wyn Wyc), Purgatory Road, Middletown
- 1882-83, Pinard Cottages, Narragansett Avenue at Annandale Road
- 1883, Jane Yardley House, 91 Rhode Island Avenue
- 1884, Ice House at Lily Pond (razed)
- 1885-87, The Cloister (James P. Kernochan House), Marine Avenue at Wetmore (razed early 1950s)
- 1885-88, Inchiquin (John O'Brien House), 719 Bellevue Avenue at Ledge Road
- 1887, Mrs. A.A. Chase House, Kay Street at Padelford Court
- 1887, Saint Joseph's Rectory (Saint Joseph's Parsonage or Parochial Residence), 39 Touro Street
- 1889-90, Lansing Zabriskie House, 90 Rhode Island Avenue

- 1890-91, Hazard Memorial School (Saint Joseph's Parochial School), behind Zion Episcopal Church (razed)
- 1890-91, Gardner S. Perry House, 280 Broadway at Newport Avenue
- 1891-95, First Presbyterian Church, 4 Everett Street
- 1892, Anthony S. Sherman House, 10 Kay Street
- 1892, Weaver Block, Broadway at Stone Street
- 1898-1900, City Hall, 43 Broadway at Bull Street (altered after fire in 1913)
- circa 1900, Wayside (Elisha Dyer House), 408 Bellevue Avenue
- 1903-05, Clingstone (Joseph Samuel Lovering Wharton House), Clingstone Island, Jamestown

renovated by John Dixon Johnston
- 1887-89, Ivy Tower (Mrs. Harriet N. Pond), 539 Bellevue Avenue (built in 1887-1888 by an unknown architect, perhaps Peabody & Stearns; renovated by Johnston in 1889 for Mrs. Charles H. Baldwin)

Patrick Charles Keeley (1816-1896)
- 1848-52, Saint Mary's Church, Spring at Memorial Boulevard
- 1864-65, Saint Mary's School House, Levin and William Streets

Charles Barton Keene (1868-1931)
- 1930, Little Clifton Berley (Windswept), 208 Ocean Avenue

Charles Eamer Kempe (1837-1907)
& Dudley Newton (1843-1907)
- 1882-87, Wakehurst (James J. Van Alen House), Ochre Point Avenue

Frederic Rhinelander King (1887-1972)
- 1918, Seamen's Church Institute, 18 Market Square
- 1921, Honyman Hall, Parish House for Trinity Church, Spring and Mill Streets
- 1921, Former Parish House for Trinity Church, High Street next to Kay Chapel
- 1927, Indian Spring (LeRoy King House), 26 Moreland Road
- 1928, Tea House (Garden House for Edith Wetmore), Chateau-sur-Mer estate, Bellevue Avenue
- 1929, Idle Hour (also called Swan's Way; Mrs. Frederic Allen House), 10 Hazard Avenue
- 1953, Sea Cliff (Reginald Rives House), 562 Bellevue Avenue

John G. Ladd
- 1836, Augustus Littlefield House (Governor Charles Van Zandt House), 70 Pelham Street

Detlef Lienau (1818-1887)
- 1852, Beach Cliffe (Delancey Kane House; later C.J. Peterson House), Bath Road at Rhode Island Avenue (razed)
- 1879-80, Anglesea (Walter Herron Lewis House; later Frederick Pearson House), Ruggles Avenue at Ochre Point Avenue

Harrie T. Lindeberg (1880–1959)
- 1926, Gray Craig (Mary and Michael van Beuren House), Gray Craig Road, Middletown

Clarence Sumner Luce (1852-1924)
- 1880-81, Mrs. Duncan Archibald Pell House (Pell-Bull-Cottrell House), 11 Francis Street
- 1880-82, Thomas R. Hunter House, 77 Rhode Island Avenue
- 1881, Aufenthalt (Mrs. Letitia B. Sargent House), 80 Kay Street
- 1881, Rear Admiral Reed Werden House, 68 Ayrault Street
- 1881, Mary & Anne Stevens House (Mrs. John Austin Stevens House), 73 Rhode Island Avenue
- 1882-83, Louisiana (Lyman C. Josephs House; now called Windemere), 438 Wolcott Avenue, Middletown
- 1882-83, The Grange (General James H. Van Alen House), Lawrence and Shepard Avenues (razed 1888)
- 1883, Miss E.G. Wilde House, 75 Kay Street
- 1883, Oakwold (Augustus Jay House), 65 Old Beach Road
- 1883, The Flower Shop (John M. Hodgson House), Bellevue Avenue at LeRoy
- 1883 Asylum, Broadway north of Equality Park (razed)
- 1883-84, Mrs. Boutelle Noyes House (Admiral Stephen B. Luce House), 15 Francis Street
- 1885-87, Reverend Henry Coit House (later Reverend J.P. Conover House), 208 Indian Avenue, Middletown

Alexander MacGregor (1796-1870)
- begun 1824, Fort Adams, Harrison Avenue
- 1831-35, Perry Mill, Thames Street at Memorial Boulevard
- 1835, Alexander MacGregor House, 63 John Street
- 1835-36, Newport Artillery Company, 23 Clarke Street
- 1845, Stone Villa (Andrew Middleton House; later James Gordon Bennett House), Bellevue Avenue at William Street (razed by 1955)
- 1851, Swanhurst (Judge Swan House), 441 Bellevue Avenue at Webster Street
- 1852-53, Stoneleigh (Dr. Benjamin Greene House; later William Thorn House; now Saint Paul's Priory), 61 Narragansett Avenue

William MacKenzie

- 1937, Seafair (Verner Z. Reed Jr. House; also called Hurricane Hut), 254 Ocean Avenue

George Champlin Mason (1820-1894)

- 1860, By-the-Sea (August Belmont House), Bellevue Avenue at Marine Avenue (razed)
- 1860, Starboard House (Edward Ogden House; later William F. Weld House), Narragansett Avenue
- 1860-61, Chepstow (Edmund Schermerhorn House), Narragansett Avenue at Clay Street
- 1860-61, Gravel Court (George B. Tiffany House), Narragansett Avenue at Clay
- 1862, Briggs House, 16 Park Street
- 1862-63, First Ward School House (Callendar School), 11 Willow Street at Third
- 1863-64, The Villa (Margaret B. Sigourney House), 437 Bellevue Avenue at Webster Street
- 1863-64, Henry Ledyard House (Thistlewaite), 44 Catherine Street at Ayrault
- 1863-64, White Lodge (Henry Sigourney House), 412 Bellevue Avenue
- circa 1864, Ray Spink House, 83 Rhode Island Avenue
- 1864-65, James C. Powell House, 72 Ayrault Street
- 1864-65, A. del Villa Yznaga House, 620 Bellevue Avenue
- 1864-65, Yznaga House, 489 Bellevue Avenue at Victoria
- 1864-65, John Carter Brown House (originally built for Henry Sigourney), 469 Bellevue Avenue at Hazard Avenue
- 1865-67, Harbor View (Ayres P. Merrill; later Stephen Whitney Phoenix House), Wellington Avenue at Chastellux Avenue (razed)
- 1866 renovation, Tillinghast Tompkins House, 11 Redwood Street
- 1866 renovation, George Thorndike House and Studio, Bellevue and Mill Streets
- 1866-67, James B. Finch House, 102 Touro Street at Mt. Vernon
- 1867, Ossory House, 15 Berkeley Street
- 1867-69, Kay Chapel, Church Street
- 1869, Rock Cliff, 670 Bellevue Avenue
- 1869-70, Edgewater (J. Frederick Kernochan Villa), foot of Webster Street (razed 1888)
- circa 1870, Sea View (James P. Kernochan House), Marine Avenue at Wetmore (razed 1875)
- 1870, Moses Lazarus House, 647 Bellevue at Lakeview
- circa 1870, Catherine Lorillard Wolfe House, Pelham and George Streets (5 Touro Park West) (extensively altered)

George Champlin Mason & Son

- 1869-70, New Lodge (Thomas F. Cushing House; later Frederick Lothrop Ames House), Bellevue Avenue (razed 1895)
- circa 1871, Misses Hazard House, 54 Kay Street
- 1871-72, Philip Case House, 60 Kay Street
- 1871-72, Mrs. Loring Andrews House, Bellevue Avenue at Bancroft (altered and later incorporated into Sherwood)
- 1871-72, Frederick Sheldon House, Annandale Road & Narragansett (razed)
- 1871-72, Edward Cunningham House (Acorn House), 1 Cottage Street
- 1871-73, Maple Shade (Dr. John R. Ogden House), 1 Red Cross Avenue
- 1872, Isaac P. White House, 66 Ayrault Street
- Cliff-Lawn (J. Winthrop Chanler House), 1872-73, Bath Road at Cliff Walk
- 1872-73, Fort Adams Commandant Quarters (for General Hunt; also called Eisenhower House), Harrison Avenue at Fort Adams
- 1872-74, Rogers High School, Church Street at School (extensively altered 1905)
- 1873-74, Heartsease (C.N. Beach House), 45 Kay Street at Ayrault
- 1873, Edward L. Brinley House, 6 Sunnyside Place
- 1873-74, Woodbine Cottage (George Champlin Mason House), 31 Old Beach Road at Sunnyside Place
- 1873-74, The Orchard (Colonel George R. Fearing House), 180 Narragansett Avenue
- 1874-75, Redwood Library Delivery Room, 50 Bellevue Avenue
- 1875, Private Residence, 20 Berkeley Street
- 1876, Cranston Street School (Cranston-Calvert School), 15 Cranston Avenue
- 1876-77, Sunset Ridge (Abiel A. Low House; later Lewis Cass Ledyard House), Ridge Road near Winans Street (razed)
- 1877, Saint John the Evangelist Church Parish House, Poplar Street
- 1877-78, Thomas Dunn House (Kate Hunter Dunn House), Coddington Cove (razed)
- 1879, The Tavern, Memorial Boulevard
- 1879-80, Seth B. Stitt House (later Countess O'Leary House; now Elks Lodge), 141 Pelham Street at Bellevue Avenue
- circa 1880, Mary Mitchell House, 13 Francis Street
- 1881, Charles Wheeler House, 247 Eustis Avenue
- 1881-82, Mrs. H.C. O'Donnell House, Ochre Point Avenue at Victoria Street (razed)

- 1882, Wol-Me (Josiah O. Low House; now called Broadlawns), 41 Ridge Road near Winans
- 1882-83, Francis Morris House, 86 Rhode Island Avenue
- 1882-83, Greystone (Fitch J. Bosworth House; later John J. Wysong House), Ochre Point Avenue
- 1882-83, Wetmore Stables, Lawrence Avenue
- 1883, George Champlin Mason Jr. House, 5 Champlin Street
- 1885-86, Saint George's Episcopal Church (new Zion Episcopal Church), 14 Rhode Island Avenue near Broadway
- 1886-88, Belmont Memorial Chapel (Island Cemetery Chapel), 30 Warner Street
- 1887-88, Swedish Methodist Episcopal Church, Annandale Road
- 1889-90, Stone Gables (Sarah Titus Zabriskie Jackson House), 100 Rhode Island Avenue
- 1889-90, Addison C. Thomas House, 96 Rhode Island Avenue
- 1891-93, Admiral Stephen B. Luce Hall (Naval War College Administration Building), Coaster's Harbor Island

Charles Follen McKim (1847-1909)
- 1874 renovation, Thomas Robinson House, 64 Washington Street
- 1875, William S. Child Schoolhouse, Second and Chestnut Streets
- 1876, Charles F. Fairchild Estate Barn, 79 Second Street at Cherry
- 1875 renovation, John Dennis House (now rectory of Saint John the Evangelist Church), 65 Poplar Street
- 1876-77, Katherine Prescott Wormeley House (Red Beach Cottage), 2 Red Cross Avenue at Old Beach Road (enlarged by McKim, Mead, and White 1882)

McKim, Mead, and White
- 1879-81, The Casino, 186-200 Bellevue Avenue
- 1880-81 addition, Kingscote Dining Room, 191 Bellevue Avenue
- 1880-82, Samuel Tilton House (later Louis Hobbs House), 12 Sunnyside Place
- 1881 addition, William Watts Sherman House Library, Shepard Avenue
- 1881-83, Isaac Bell House (Edna Villa), Bellevue Avenue
- 1881-83, William Starr Miller House, Bellevue Avenue
- 1882, Villino (Mrs. Frances L. Skinner House), 6 Red Cross Avenue
- 1882-83, Samuel Colman House (Whileaway), 7 Red Cross Avenue
- 1882-83, Charles M. Bull House, One Mile Corner (West Main Road) (razed)

- 1882-84, Ochre Point (Robert Goelet House; incorrectly called Southside), Narragansett Avenue at 40 Steps
- 1884-86, Commodore William Edgar House (Sunnyside), 29 Old Beach Road at Sunnyside Place
- 1884-86, Berkeley Villa (LeRoy King House), 324 Bellevue Avenue at Berkeley Street
- 1884-86, Henry Augustus Coit Taylor House, Annandale Road at Ward Street (razed after 1952)
- 1886-87, Berry Hill (John H. Glover House), Hammersmith Road
- 1887-88, Edgehill (George Gordon King House), Harrison Avenue
- 1888-91, Beacon Rock (Edwin Dennison Morgan III House), 147 Harrison Avenue
- 1897-1902, Rosecliff (Hermann and Theresa Fair (Tessie) Oelrichs House), 548 Bellevue Avenue
- 1924, Schoolhouse, Saint George's School (adjoining Chapel), Purgatory Road, Middletown
- 1929, Miantonomi Tower, Admiral Kalbfus Road, Middletown

Charles Merry
- 1883-84, Dr. Christopher M. Bell House, Bellevue Avenue north of Marine (razed)

Miller & Greene
- 1881, Mrs. K.R. Breese House, 48 Everett Street

Richard Munday (d. 1739)
- 1725-26, Trinity Church, Spring Street at Church
- 1739-44, Colony House (the State House after Revolutionary War), Washington Square

Attributed to Richard Munday (d. 1739)
- circa 1720, Jalheel Brenton House, Thames Street (old wide line) (razed 1920s)
- 1727-28, Abraham Redwood City Mansion, Thames Street near Perry Mill (razed circa 1850)
- 1727-28, Godfrey Malbone City Mansion, Thames Street near Perry Mill (razed circa 1850)
- 1729-30, Seventh Day Baptist Meeting House (now incorporated into the Newport Historical Society), 82 Touro Street

Dudley Newton (1843-1907)

- circa 1800 renovation, Oakland Farm (Cornelius Vanderbilt II Country House), Portsmouth (razed 1947-50)
- 1865, Saint Spyridon Greek Orthodox Church, 390 Thames Street
- circa 1865, Twin Half Houses, 22 and 22 1/2 Kay Street
- 1866-67, Police Station (Market Square Police Station), Thames Street at Market Square (razed 1914)
- 1866-67, Chastellux (Lorillard Spencer House), Chastellux (King) Avenue
- 1867, Dr. J.R. Newton Office and Residence, 392 Thames Street
- 1867, Engine House for Steamer #2, 119 Touro Street at Mary Street (razed 1895)
- 1870 renovation, Belair, 34 Old Beach Road (original house by Seth Bradford, 1850)
- 1871-72, Benjamin H. Rhodes House, 45 Everett Street
- 1872, King-Birckhead House, 20 Catherine Street
- 1872, Dudley Newton Office and Studio, 20 Bellevue Avenue
- 1872 renovation, Residence, 21 Kay Street
- circa 1872, French Mansard House, 204 Spring Street
- 1873, Captain C.C. Churchill House (later Rear Admiral Harry E. Yarnell House), 62 Ayrault Street
- 1873-74, Thames Street Methodist Episcopal Church, Thames Street (razed)
- 1874, John Downing, Malbone Road
- 1874-75, Newport Gas Company, Thames Street (razed)
- 1875 and 1880 additions, Muenchinger-King House, 34-38 Bellevue Avenue
- 1875, Belair Stable, 34 Old Beach Road
- 1875, Belair Porter's Lodge, 34 Old Beach Road
- 1875-76, Henry T. Swinburne House, 97 Rhode Island Avenue
- 1875-76, Mrs. George Clarence Cram House (later Jacob Cram House; later Mary Sturtevant House), Abe Meyer Way off Purgatory Road, Middletown
- 1875-76, Sarah C. Woolsey House, 93 Rhode Island Avenue
- 1875-76, French Mansard House, 92 Rhode Island Avenue
- 1878-79, William H. Smith House (now Rectory of Channing Memorial), 135 Pelham Street
- 1880, John T. Bush House, Division Street
- 1880-81, Convent for the Sisters of Mercy (Saint Mary's Church Convent), Spring Street
- 1880-81, Charles Pinard House, 49 Annandale Road
- 1881-82, Sunnylea (Charles F. Chickering House), 541 Bellevue Avenue
- 1882, Dudley Newton House, 52 Division Street
- 1882, Thomas Brown House, 21 Ayrault Street
- 1882-83, Ochre Lodge (Miss Julia Eldridge House), Ruggles and Lawrence Avenues
- 1882-83, Henrietta Lieber House, 67 Rhode Island Avenue
- 1882-83, Matilda Lieber House, 69 Rhode Island Avenue
- 1882-84, Hawkhurst (Caroline Seymour House), divided into four segments at 66 Kay Street, 68 Kay Street, 70 Kay Street, and 39-41 Cranston Avenue
- 1882-84, William G. Weld House (De La Salle), 364 Bellevue Avenue
- 1883-84, Bethsan (Major Theodore Kane Gibbs House), 396 Gibbs Avenue
- 1883-84, William Binney House (later Catherine H. Hunt; called Windecke), 80 Catherine Street
- circa 1885, Stable Complex, Coggeshall Avenue
- 1888-89, Wakehurst Stables (James J. Van Alen Stables), Shepard Avenue
- 1891-93, Kinsley Building (Aquidneck Bank/Kinsley Block), Thames Street at Pelham
- 1893-94, Harold Carter Brown Villa & Stable, Bellevue Avenue at Hazard Avenue
- 1895, Newport Fire Station No. 5, 119 Touro Street at Mary
- 1897, Susan Weaver House, 59 Kay Street at Everett Street
- 1897-98, Crossways (Stuyvesant Fish House), Ocean Avenue at Jeffrey Road

Noel & Miller (G. Macculoch Miller)

- 1939, Gertrude Vanderbilt Whitney Studio, 562 Bellevue and Cliff Walk

Alexander F. Oakey

- 1882-83, J. Griffiths Masten House, 43 Everett Street

Cotton Palmer

- 1729, First Congregational Church, Mill Street at Division Street
- 1735, Second Congregational Church (Second Baptist Church), Clarke Street

Peabody & Stearns

- circa 1871, Frederick S.C. D'Hauteville House, Bellevue Avenue at Gordon(razed)
- 1871-72, Nathan Matthews House (later James R. Keene House), Bellevue Avenue at Victoria (burned 1881)
- 1872, Weetamore (George Wheatland House; later Nathaniel Thayer Cottage), 643 Bellevue Avenue at Rovensky
- 1876-77, Grace W. Rives House (Hambly Funeral Home), 30 Red Cross Avenue

- 1877-78, The Breakers (Pierre Lorillard House), Ruggles Avenue (burned 1892)
- circa 1880, Laurelawn (Mrs. Frances Murdoch House), 590 Bellevue Avenue
- 1882-83, Arthur D. Emmons House, 125 Gibbs Avenue
- 1882-83, Vinland (Catherine Lorillard Wolfe House; later Mrs. Hamilton Twombly House), Ochre Point Avenue
- 1882-83, Vinland Stables (for Catherine Lorillard Wolfe), Ochre Point Avenue
- 1884-85, Vinland Farmhouse and Hennery (for Catherine Lorillard Wolfe), 137 Webster Street
- 1885-86, The Breakers Playhouse (for Pierre Lorillard), Ochre Point Avenue
- 1886, Honeysuckle Lodge (Joseph M. Fiske House; later T. Suffern Tailer House; also called Masonlea), Ruggles Avenue
- 1886, Mid-Cliff (Caroline Ogden Jones and Louis B. McCagg House), Ruggles Avenue
- 1886-87, Bathing Pavilion, Easton's or First Beach (destroyed 1938)
- 1887-91, Rough Point (Frederick William Vanderbilt House; later Doris Duke House), 680 Bellevue Avenue
- 1888-89, Ocean Lawn (Mrs. William Gammell House), Cliff Walk near Annandale Road
- 1889-90, Althorpe (John Thompson Spencer House), Ruggles Avenue
- 1890-91, 1893, 1895-96, Rockhurst (Mrs. H. Mortimer Brooks House), 720 Bellevue Avenue at Ledge Road (razed)
- 1892-93, Second Bleak House (Ross R. Winans House), 551 Ocean Avenue near Winans Avenue (razed)
- 1893-95, Beechbound (William Burden House), 127 Harrison Avenue
- 1894-96, Shamrock Cliff (Ocean Cliff; Gawn Hutton House), Ridge Road
- 1897-98, Ridgemere (Fanny Foster House), LeRoy Avenue
- 1899-1902, Hopedene (Elizabeth H.G. Slater House), Cliff Walk (Annandale Road)
- 1907-10, Vinland Caretaker's Cottage (for Mrs. Hamilton Twombly House), Ochre Point Avenue

E. Truman Peckham (d. 1913)
- 1875, Paradise School, Paradise Avenue, Middletown

Job Peckham
- 1855, John Irish House, 26 Kay Street
- circa 1855, Joseph Bailey House, 30 Kay Street
- circa 1855, Job Peckham House, 33 Kay Street

Charles Adams Platt (1861-1933)
- 1927, Bois Dore (William Fahnestock House), Narragansett Avenue

George Platt
- 1864-65, Paran Stevens House, Bellevue Avenue at Jones and King Streets (razed by 1955)

Polhemus & Coffin
- 1929, Champ Soleil (Mrs. Drexel Dahlgren House), 601 Bellevue Avenue

John Russell Pope (1874-1937)
- 1901-03, Whiteholme (Dr. and Mrs. Henry Barton Jacobs Estate), Ochre Point Avenue (razed circa 1960)
- 1912-18, Bonniecrest (Stuart Duncan House), 117 Harrison Avenue
- 1920-22, Moses Taylor House (Glen Farm), East Main Road, Middletown
- 1927-29, The Waves (John Russell Pope House), Ledge Road

George Browne Post (1837-1913)
- 1880-81, Chateau-Nooga (Christopher Columbus Baldwin House), 420 Bellevue Avenue at Narragansett

Potter & Robertson
- 1877-78, Charles H. Baldwin House (Garmirdoon, later Prescott Lawrence House), 328 Bellevue Avenue

William Appleton Potter (1842-1909)
- 1882-85, Stoneacre (John W. Ellis House), Bellevue Avenue at Victoria Street (burned 1953)
- 1882-85, Stoneacre Carriage House (John W. Ellis Dependency), Ruggles Avenue at Ruggles Street

Powel & Spencer
- 1852-53, Samuel Powel House (George Merrill House; also called Merillton), Bowery Street at King

Samuel F. Pratt
- 1871-72, Samuel F. Pratt House (Bird's Nest Cottage), 49 Bellevue Avenue at Redwood Street

Bruce Price (1843-1903)
- circa 1895, Belmead (Frederick W. Vanderbilt II House), 529 Bellevue Avenue at Ruggles
- 1903, Audrain Building, 220-230 Bellevue Avenue

James Renwick Jr. (1818-1895)
- 1883-85, East Court (George G. Haven House), 337 Bellevue Avenue at Bellevue Court

Henry Hobson Richardson (1838-1886)
- 1872-73, Frank W. Andrews House (Sunset Lawn), Maple Avenue, Coddington Cove, Middletown (razed 1920s)
- 1874-75, William Watts Sherman House, Shepard Avenue
- 1882-83 renovation, Misses Mason House, 100 Rhode Island Avenue (original house by Seth C. Bradford, circa 1850) (burned 1899)
- 1889-90 (after his design), Castle Hill Lighthouse, 600 Ocean Avenue at Castle Hill

Robert H. Robertson (1849-1919)
- 1887-89, Hammersmith Farm (John W. Auchincloss House), Harrison Avenue
- 1898-09, The Breakwater (Governor Charles W. Lippitt House), Ledge Road (razed 1924)

Attributed to Andrew Robeson Jr.
- 1852-53, Elm Court (The Cedars; later Frank Work House), 245 Bellevue Avenue at West Bowery Street

Isaiah Rogers
- 1842, Touro Cemetery Gates, 2 Bellevue Avenue

Philip Simmons or Richard Upjohn
- 1850-51, Ocean Lawn (Hon. Robert H. Ives House; later Mrs. Elizabeth Gammell), Narragansett Avenue at Cliff Walk (moved in 1888)

Robert H. Slack
- 1874-75, Castle Hill (Alexander Agassiz House), Ocean Avenue

Joseph Southwick
- circa 1840, Round House, Southwick's Grove, Forest Avenue, Middletown (razed)

Rev. E.A. Stanley
- 1870-71, Sea-View Cottages, Cliff Walk near Cliff Avenue

John Hubbard Sturgis (1834-1888) (Sturgis & Brigham)
- 1863-64, Frederick W. Rhinelander House, 10 Redwood Street
- 1864-65, Greenvale Farm (John S. Barstow House), Wapping Road, Portsmouth
- 1866-68, The Rocks (Edward Darley Boit Jr. House; later Henry Clews House), 64 Ocean Avenue (razed)
- 1864-65, Land's End (Samuel G. Ward House; later Edith Wharton House), 42 Ledge Road
- 1867, The Ledges (Robert M. Cushing House), 66 Ocean Avenue
- 1876-78, John Carey Garden Cottage, 523 Spring Street
- circa 1880, Professor Oliver Wolcott Gibbs House, 316 Gibbs Avenue
- 1882-83, The Reef (Theodore M. Davis; later Milton Budlong House), 501 Ocean Avenue (burned)

Thomas Alexander Tefft (1826-1859)
- 1853, Joseph Tompkins House, 38 Catherine Street
- 1853-54, Quatrel (Earl P. Mason House; also called Fairbourne), 669 Bellevue Avenue (extensively altered)

Joseph Totten with Alexander MacGregor
- 1824-57, Fort Adams, Brenton's Reef

Horace Trumbauer (1869-1938)
- 1899-1902, The Elms (Edward Julius Berwind House), 350 Bellevue Avenue
- 1900-03, Chetwode (William Storrs Wells House), Bellevue Avenue at Ruggles (razed 1973)
- 1903-04, Clarendon Court (Edward C. Knight House, originally called Claradon Court; later Claus Von Bulow House), 620 Bellevue Avenue at Rovensky Street
- 1912-14, Miramar (Mrs. George Widener House; later Alexander Hamilton Rice House), 650 Bellevue Avenue
- 1925, Stonybrook, 501 Indian Avenue

Richard Upjohn (1802-1878)

- 1839-41, Kingscote (George Noble Jones House; later William Henry King House), 191 Bellevue Avenue at Bowery
- 1845, Church of the Holy Cross, West Main Road at Oliphant Lane
- 1845-47, Edward King House, Spring Street at West Bowery Street
- 1847, Saint Mary's Episcopal Church, 324 East Main Road, Portsmouth
- 1852-53, Oak-Lawn (Charles Handy Russell House), 424 Bellevue Avenue at Narragansett (razed 1887)
- 1855-56, Old Emmanuel Church, Spring Street at Dearborn (razed 1902)
- 1856-57, Hamilton Hoppin House (Shadow Lawn), Miantonomi Avenue, Middletown
- 1857-58, Alexander Van Rensselaer House (called Restmere and Villalou), Miantonomi Avenue, Middletown

Calvert Vaux (1824-1892)

- 1852-53, Beechwood (Daniel Parrish House; later Mrs. Caroline Backhouse Astor House), 580 Bellevue Avenue
- 1856-59, Beaulieu (Frederick L. de Barreda House; later William Tilden Blodgett House), 614 Bellevue Avenue (extensively altered)
- 1880-81, Raphael Pumpelly House, 288 Gibbs Avenue (burned 1920)
- 1883-84, Boothden (Edwin Booth House), 357 Indian Avenue, Middletown

William Russell Walker (1830-1905)

- 1866, Ocean View (Mr. and Mrs. Ogden Mills House), 662 Bellevue Avenue

Russell Warren (1792-1860)

- 1829, Custom's House (Old Post Office), Thames Street (razed)
- 1833, Saint Paul's Episcopal Church, 2679 East Main Road, Portsmouth
- 1833-35, Elmhyrst (William Vernon House), One Mile Corner, Middletown
- 1834, Zion Episcopal Church (later Strand Theatre and now Jane Pickens Theatre), Touro Street at Clarke (extensively altered)
- 1834, North Baptist Church (also called Second Baptist Church), North Baptist Street (razed)

- 1834, Levi H. Gale House, 85 Touro at Division Street
- 1845, Second Ocean House, Bellevue Avenue at Bowery (burned 1898)

Attributed to Russell Warren (1792-1860)

- circa 1835, Hon. William Beach Lawrence House, Lawrence Avenue (razed 1882)
- 1840-44, Atlantic House, Bellevue Avenue at Pelham Street (razed 1877)
- 1840-44, First Ocean House, Bellevue Avenue at Bowery (burned 1845)

Whitney Warren (1864-1943)

- 1894-95, Newport Country Club Clubhouse, Harrison Avenue
- 1900, High Tide (William Starr Miller House), 79 Ocean Avenue

Joseph C. Wells

- 1852-53, Rose Cliff (George Bancroft House), 548 Bellevue Avenue north of Marine (razed 1897)
- 1852-53, Sea Cliffe (The Reefs) (Christopher Wolfe House; later John Knower House; later Harry Payne Whitney House), 562 Bellevue Avenue at Bancroft (burned 1942)
- 1855-57, United Congregational Church (now Newport Congregational Church), Spring Street at Pelham

Edward Payson Whitman

- 1905, Castlewood (Louis Bruguiere House; later The Mercy Home & School), Tonomy Hill, Middletown (razed)

William F. Wilbor

- circa 1880, Private Residence, 7 Rhode Island Avenue
- 1881, William F. Wilbor House, 9 Rhode Island Avenue

Edwin Wilbur

- 1894, Newport Guard Armory Building, 371 Thames Street

Frederick Clarke Withers (1828-1901)

- 1894, Saint John the Evangelist Church (Sarah T. Zabriskie Memorial), Washington Street at Willow Street

Woodcock & Meacham

- 1864-65, Perry House Hotel, Washington Square (razed 1920s)

(List courtesy of Professor James Yarnall)

architectural styles

Colonial, 1639–1789

Early Organic, 1840–1870

Federal, 1780–1810

Cottage Ornée, 1850–1870

Greek Revival, 1810–1840

Chalet, 1850–1875

Stick, 1860–1880

Shingle, 1875–1885

Italianate, 1860–1880

Queen Anne, 1875–1885

maps and illustrations

1. View of Newport, pencil drawing, RG

3. Newport City Hall, pencil drawing, RG

4. Vernon Court, watercolor, RG

8. Newport Harbor and Trinity, watercolor, RG

9. Self-portrait of Gilbert Stuart, Redwood Library

11. Old Stone Mill, pencil drawing, RG

12–13. Blaskowitz Map of 1777, detail

14. Blaskowitz Map of 1777, detail

15. Portion of Print, *Harper's Weekly,* August 30, 1873

15. View of Spring Street, pencil drawing, RG

16. Wanton Lyman Hazard House, pencil, RG

17. Colonial Framing, pencil, RG

17. Mortise and Tenon Joint, pencil, RG

18. Lucina Langley House, pencil, RG

19. John Bliss House, pencil, RG

21. Easton's Pond, map

22. View of Newport Beach, photo, NHS

22. Print of Old Newport, NHS

24. Framed Overhang, Sueton-Grant House, pencil, RG

24–25. Colonial Roof Types, pencil, RG

25. The White Horse Tavern, watercolor, RG

26. Trinity Church and Church Street, watercolor, RG

27. Blaskowitz Map of the Point

28. The Hunter House, pencil, RG

30. Trinity Tower, watercolor, RG

30. Pulpit, Trinity Church, pencil, RG

31. Colony House, watercolor, RG

32. Redwood Library, watercolor, RG

33. The Brick Market, watercolor, RG

33. Touro Synagogue, watercolor, RG

35. Blaskowitz Map of Narragansett Bay

36. General John Sullivan, oil portrait

37. Map of Goat Island

37. Officers' Houses on Goat Island, pencil, RG

38. Vernon House, watercolor, RG

40. Monticello, pencil, RG

41. St. Paul's, watercolor, RG

41. Federal Style, St. Paul's, Pattern Book, illustration

42. Robert Lawton House, watercolor, RG

42. The Whitehorne Museum, watercolor, RG

43. Elmhyrst, watercolor, RG

44. Map of John, Pelham, and Mill streets

45. Greek Revival Plan

45. The Golden Mean

46. Postcard, Elmhyrst

46–47. Elmhyrst, watercolor, RG

48. 115 Pelham Street, watercolor, RG

48. Clarke Street Church, photo, NHS

49. Second Congregational Church, pencil, RG

50. Washington Street Skyline, pencil, RG

51. Newport Waterfront in the 1800s, NHS

52. Perry Mill, pencil, RG

53. Fort Adams, Eastern Wall, watercolor, RG

54. Newport Skyline, *Harper's Weekly,* August 30, 1873

54. Fort Adams, aerial photo

55. Fort Adams, plan

56. Lansmere, watercolor, RG

57. St. Mary's Church, watercolor, RG

58. Halidon Hall, watercolor, RG

59. Swanhurst, watercolor, RG

60. Kingscote, watercolor, RG

61. Atlantic House, watercolor, RG

62. Ocean House, print

63. Ocean House, pencil, RG

63. Locations of Hotels, map

64. Atlantic House, print

64. Bellevue House, pencil, RG

65. Bellevue Avenue, map

65. Old Beach Road Neighborhood, maps, RIPC

67. Thomas Cushing House, watercolor, RG

68. Benjamin Marsh House, pencil, RG

69. Griswold House, pencil, RG

70. Samuel Pratt House, pencil, RG

71. Samuel Pratt House, watercolor, RG

72. Edward King House, watercolor, RG

73. Bienvenu, pencil, RG

74. The Chalet on Halidon Hill, watercolor, RG

75. Frederick Rhinelander House, watercolor, RG

76. Mrs. Loring Andrews House, photo

78. Watts Sherman House, ink, PPL

79. Stanford White sketch of Watts Sherman House

79. C.C. Baldwin House, pencil, RG

80–81. Isaac Bell House, watercolor, RG

83. W.G. Weld House, pencil, RG

84. Heartsease, photo

85. George Champlin Mason House, pencil, RG

86. Fort Adams Commandant Headquarters, watercolor, RG

86. Chateau-sur-Mer, pencil, RG

87. Jeremiah Stitts House, watercolor, RG

87. Sarah Zabriskie House, pencil, RG

88. Dudley Newton Studio, pencil, RG

89. Jacob Cram House, watercolor, RG

89. Belair Carriage House, pencil, RG

90. Henry Swinburne House, watercolor, RG

91. William Smith House, watercolor, RG

92. Hawkhurst, photo, NHS

92. Bethshan, watercolor, RG

93. Four Buildings, Hawkhurst, pencil, RG

94. Dudley Newton Studio, detail, pencil, RG

95. William Smith House and Channing Memorial Church, pencil, RG

97. Watts Sherman House, watercolor, RG

98. Frank Andrews House, pencil, RG

101. Plan of Andrews House, 1872

102. Watts Sherman House, watercolor, RG

103. Castle Hill Light, H.H. Richardson

104. Linden Gate, pencil, RG

105. Griswold House, watercolor, RG

107. Plan of the Griswold House

108–109. Katherine Wormeley House, watercolor, RG

110. Frances L. Skinner House, pencil, RG

110. Samuel Coleman House, watercolor, RG

111. Tilton House, watercolor, RG

112. Newport Casino, pencil, RG

112. Newport Casino, pencil, RG

113. Isaac Bell House, watercolor, RG

113. Commodore Edgar House, pencil, RG

115. Bellevue Avenue, Iron Fence, watercolor, RG

116. Map of Bellevue Houses

117. Lamp on Bellevue Avenue, watercolor, RG

118. Lamp, pencil, RG

119. Vernon Court, watercolor, RG

120. Ochre Court, pencil, RG

121. Belcourt, pencil, RG

122. The Breakers, pencil, RG

123. Marble House, pencil, RG

124. The Chinese Tea House, watercolor, RG

125. Rosecliff, pencil, RG

126. The Elms, pencil, RG

127. Beacon Rock, watercolor, RG

129. Ridgemere, pencil, RG

130. Olmsted's Newport

135. Bonniecrest, pencil, RG

136. Bonniecrest, detail, pencil, RG

137. The Waves, watercolor, RG

138. St. Michael's School, watercolor, RG

139. Wildacre, watercolor, RG

140. St. George's School Tower, pencil, RG

140. Emmanuel Church, pencil, RG

141. St. George's School, watercolor, RG

142–143. St. George's School, from Second Beach, oil, RG

Credits

RG: Richard Grosvenor

NHS: Newport Historical Society

RIPC: Rhode Island Preservation Commission

PPL: Providence Public Library

acknowledgments

This book is really a compendium of information gleaned from innumerable sources at odd times in my life, especially during the period that I was teaching at St. George's School, from 1953 to 1993. As head of the art department, I initiated a course in architecture, with special emphasis on Newport. At that time, I read extensively from the *Architectural Heritage of Newport, Rhode Island,* by Antoinette Downing and Vincent Scully. Many years ago when I first had the idea to write this book, I conferred a great deal with Mrs. Gladys Bolhouse of the Newport Historical Society, Mr. King Covell of Washington Street, and Mr. William Warren of Jamestown. They were very helpful, especially by sharing with me their photographic collections. Now all those people have passed on, but they might be pleased to know that I appreciated their help. Mr. John Hopf helped extensively with photographs and general advice on all subjects. Innumerable people gave me access to their homes, as well as encouragement, during this architectural quest. Many others, too numerous to mention, enabled my students to learn about architecture by allowing them to measure their houses for the construction of models—the first project of each academic year. I would like to mention, however, the generosity of the Tournquists, as I believe their home, the Bliss House, served as a model for the students perhaps four or five times. The Redwood graciously allowed me to display my students' house models in the library every year. Thanks, also, to all the staff of Trinity Church, and especially to Herb Lawton, who allowed me and my students to climb the tower and study the hand-hewn beams in the very heart of the structure. Many others helped, especially the staff of the Redwood Library; Richard Champlin gave me advice and straightened me out historically, when I needed it, and more recently, I am grateful for the assistance of Cheryl Helms, Maris Humphreys and Linda Bronaugh as well as Robert Behra. Also, the Redwood Library graciously allowed me to display my students' house models every year. I mention all this in the context of teaching at St. George's, because it was that experience that gave me the inspiration to write this book. Another inspiration

who should not be forgotten is my late friend Clarkson Potter, who told me that the book was worth publishing and who indeed acted as my agent for several years. Alas, we had little success, but his confidence was a driving force.

The Newport Historical Society has been one of my main sources of information. Dan Snydacker, the director, has been most helpful, and his staff has given me support, help and assistance. Joan Youngken, the curator of photographs, has a vast knowledge of the Society's collection, and her aid in coming up with the right picture has been truly wonderful. Bert Lippincott, the librarian, has supplied me with the proper material, as did Ron Potvin and, in short, the whole group has been a strong, positive force in this project.

As far as a truly outstanding resource, I want to thank Ned Reynolds, a former student, who did a college thesis on Newport architect Dudley Newton. Ned allowed me to use the information that he laboriously assembled as a basis for the portion that I wrote on that architect. Another person who has given me a lot of professional help is Paul Miller, curator of the Preservation Society of Newport, who has an acute interest in the history of Newport and is second to none in his knowledge of the facts and personalities of the nineteenth century. Other people that I would like to thank include Frank Girr, who has always kept me supplied with photocopies of interesting sidelights in the history of Newport, and Bob Fagan, who has kept me abreast of the findings that he has gleaned about Newport through Salve Regina University's connection with the Internet and the Library of Congress. Also, thanks to Brett McKenzie for bringing this book to the attention of Don Gardiner, president of the Rhode Island Historical Society, who in turn presented it to Webster Bull of Commonwealth Editions who enabled it to see the light of day. Also, many thanks for the invaluable editing done initially by Susan Ryan, later by Betty Hackman, then Shawna Mullen, and finally, Jay Donahue, and my daughter-in-law Terry Grosvenor. Jim Yarnall, chairman of the Art Department at Salve Regina University spent a great deal of time with me editing the manuscript and adding his information for me to use in the listing of Newport architects in the final appendix. I am most grateful to him. Thanks, too, to Mack Woodward of the Rhode Island Historical Preservation & Heritage Commission for his expert reading.

The greatest inspiration of all were my wife, Margot, who is a source of encouragement as well as a tough critic—both of immeasurable value—and our children. My son Rick and his wife, Terry, made a huge contribution of time and computer expertise, two elements critical in putting this book together. Rick's work included scanning every image here. Their important help came at moments that I know were inconvenient to them, but they came through anyway. My son John's essay, first printed in *Newport Life* magazine, served as a source for the information printed here on Alexander MacGregor. As successful architects, John and my daughter Holly both gave me important advice along the way. Our youngest son, Jim, sent supportive wishes from far off California and, more recently, New York. To all those near and dear, thank you.